PLAYING IN DIRT

PLAYING IN DIRT

A FAMILY'S FAITHFUL JOURNEY IN BATTLING CHILDHOOD CANCER

KIMBERLEY GHIGGIA THORN

For information contact:
kim@authorkimberleythorn.com

Published by:
Boone Springs Publishing

Cover design and interior book design by
Francine Platt, Eden Graphics, Inc.

Cover background photo: istockphoto • Creativeye99

Family photos on cover, back cover, and throughout the book
are by Betty Ghiggia and Jerry Pierce

Hardback ISBN 979-8-89454-118-1
Paperback ISBN 979-8-89454-119-8
eBook ISBN 979-8-89454-120-4
Audiobook ISBN 979-8-89454-121-1

Library of Congress Control Number: 2026905405

Manufactured in the United States of America

First Edition

*For my mom,
my biggest cheerleader.*

SPECIAL THANKS

Writing this book has helped me to fully embrace how eternally grateful I am for the people God has placed in my life, especially in my younger years when it took a village to help raise me. I have deep appreciation to those of you who walked with me during my childhood. You each were a very important piece in the puzzle of my life and you will always hold a special place in my heart.

To my family, you are the glue that holds us all together when life falls apart. Thank you to my mom, Betty, for teaching me how to embrace and persevere through life's many challenges, to my dad, Gene, for helping me learn ways to find joy in everything, to my big brother, Clint, for showing me that life is meant to be lived, and to my little brother, Cody, for being the light on our darkest days.

Special thanks to my husband, Michael, for endless conversations about my book, for listening as I spent countless hours reminiscing about my past, and for compassionately interjecting ideas at moments when I couldn't quite formulate my thoughts into words. Thank you for your unwavering support, dedication, and commitment. You are my anchor.

To my extended family, loved ones and friends, thank you for providing encouragement throughout my life and for offering insightful feedback over the course of this book writing process. I am grateful to each one of you and your unwavering support.

Grandma Thorn, Grandma Renslow, and Miss Myrtle, thank you for your genuine interest in my childhood, our family trials, your constant prayers and encouragement during some of our darkest hours, and for listening with your whole heart. You all came to mind several times as I was writing this book. In those moments I imagined you all sitting close by hearing my heart pour onto the pages.

Thank you to my students; past and present. You are the reason that I write. You are the reason that I share my thoughts. You are my inspiration. Never forget how important you are to me!

Richard Paul Evans and the Author Ready Program, thank you for doing what you do. You were my guide many years before I even considered jumping into this book writing journey.

A heartfelt thank you to Debbie Rasmussen, my content editor, for leading me every step of the way through the publishing process. I'll never forget how nervous I was to share this book with someone besides my mom. Your tenderness and encouragement helped me to navigate the waters and bring this project to fruition. The moments that we laughed and cried together during late nights of editing, as we read through memories of me being five years old, will forever be etched in my book of life. Thank you for those moments. You are a special soul.

Thank you to my copy editor, Kim Autrey, for your insight and perspective on the final written copy of this book. I appreciate your expertise.

Francine Platt, from the bottom of my heart, thank you for all your hard work, the countless hours you spent designing the book cover and finalizing the interior design of this book. I am grateful for everything you did to make this book beautiful. You are a special treasure.

Above all else, thank you, Jesus, for never leaving my side. Even at times when I feel that I am all alone, you subtly remind me that you are always there. I can't imagine living this life without you. You are the light of the world.

MY HOME

I don't live in a castle,
Nor a shining sea.
I don't live on the moon,
And the city's not for me.
Where I live is just a house
Filled with laughter, you can hear
And even when I'm far away
I feel that I am near.

By: Kimberley Ghiggia
Age 9

Home is where I've always found happiness. I wrote this poem with the encouragement of my fourth grade teacher Ms. Littlefield and the guidance of my mom, who has always been an amazing poet. This poem was published in a book, my first ever published writing, after it won first place in a nationwide writing contest in 1987.

Growing up with a brother who had cancer could have been a life full of doom and gloom, but for our family, we always found joy in the struggle. I sometimes wonder what it would be like to live in a world where you didn't have to worry about things like bills, cancer, and death. Most parents try to shelter their young children from such worries. My parents had no choice but to share these realities with me before I could even talk. I have never known a world without such worries, and I'm not sure that I'd want it any other way. For it is in the struggles of life that I found unexplainable joy, complete happiness, and an abundance of love. It's in darkness where the light shone the brightest. Though my family and I were very close and shared the same struggles, no two people remember things exactly the same. Every person has their own story, their own perspective on things, their own memories. This is how I remember it...

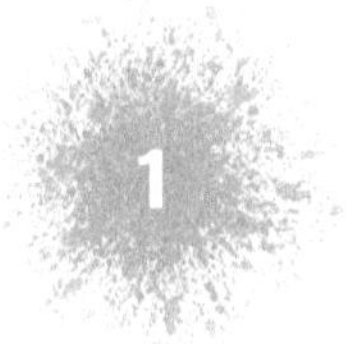

FINDING OUR WAY

THERE I WAS, five years old, surrounded by fog so thick I imagined I could cut it with a knife. Sometimes the tule fog settled in California's Central Valley for days on end.

It was cold, wet, and, according to my mom, depressing. I had no idea what *depressing* was then, but I did know the fog made me feel trapped, like I was being swallowed up by a giant sea of white that was impossible to swim in. On days like these we bundled up in our warmest jackets and embraced the damp clouds. We hoped we wouldn't get lost before we made it to our destination.

It was still dark, and I couldn't even see my brother, who was just a few feet ahead of me. I followed his footsteps along the dirt trail on the edge of the almond orchard that led to the bus stop. He would be waiting for me there.

We usually walked on the paved country road between the almond orchard and my great-grandparents' grape vineyard. But today the fog was so thick, we traipsed along in the dirt so we wouldn't get hit by a car. On other days, when we did walk on the road, we had plenty of time to get out of the way of any vehicle that might be remotely close to us.

That day, I hugged close to the large almond trees; I wasn't about to take any chances!

I'm not sure how early it was, but if it had been a Saturday, my brother and I would have still been in our pajamas watching the Saturday morning cartoons on TV.

The world was starting to stir. The farmers were probably up drinking their coffee, the newspaper man just finishing up his route, throwing papers out his car window, and by now, the kids that lived out in the country were waiting for the bus to pick them up. It may have been around 6:30 a.m. on that cold, November morning.

I finally made it to where my brother was patiently waiting for me. Our bus stop was a single red sign on the corner where one street collided with another. It was less than ten minutes away from our house, but that morning it felt like a hundred miles.

The stop sign was our mighty protector on days like these. It would watch over us while we waited patiently for the bus to rescue us from whatever weather prevailed. The moisture in the air encapsulated the fall country smell; a distinct mixture of damp almond tree bark, firewood smoke that lingered from fireplaces, soaked grape leaves that still hung on the vines, and wet dirt. So much dirt.

My brother and I listened closely to every noise that entered our little world. We counted down the seconds that it took each sound to reach us. First, a pickup truck filled with kids. When we heard it, we watched it roll through the stop sign, envious of the cab that was keeping the family warm. Next, a train way off in the distance, muffled by the dense fog, the echo still carried for miles.

The fog had a way of blanketing the sounds making it hard to distinguish where they were coming from. Next, nothing at all, just absolute silence.

There we were, my big brother and I, waiting for the big, yellow school bus to rescue us when it arrived at *our* stop sign. We passed the time telling each other stories and playing in the dirt with our feet. We had a little game that we often played called, *Indian Bowl.* We took pride in our game, imagining that our Native American ancestors had once played it, though I'm guessing that they didn't.

The goal was to see who could make the largest *bowl* in the dirt by using just our feet. From watching my brother, I learned very quickly that there was a special technique to the bowl making. It was all in moving the heel. First, we had to find dirt that wasn't too soft or too hard. Since the area where we lived in the Central Valley of California had near-perfect planting soil, this task wasn't difficult. We found dirt that was packed down just enough to be strong, then pressed the heel of our foot deep into the soil. The rest was easy and fun. We would twirl our bodies round and round with our heel still firmly planted in the ground creating a dirt bowl.

I dug my heel into the dirt and pointed my toes toward the sky. The dirt was perfect that morning because the fall moisture in the air had moistened it just enough to make it compact. I spun in a circle, pivoting my heel so that it created a hole with each spin of my body. The more I pressed with my heel, the deeper the bowl got. After several minutes of this motion, my brother and I checked to see whose hole was deeper.

His bowl was always deeper than mine. I was sure he must have cheated in some way. Usually, after a few attempts at making my bowl deeper, I grew bored with the game, and this morning was no exception. I quickly saw that my brother's was already double the size of mine, so I changed up the game and began making as many small ones as I could. He might have been able to make the deepest bowl, but I was determined to make more than he did. I did this while imagining that I was preparing a feast for family and friends who would join me to eat something delicious out of each one. No matter what the game was, playing in the dirt was always fun. My brother continued making his deeper, trying to be a champion of the deepest hole ever dug with the heel of a foot. I didn't mind him winning at the deepest bowl game. That made him happy, which in turn made me happy too.

Suddenly, we heard the sound that only a child can hear from miles away. Like Santa Claus on the rooftop on Christmas Eve; it brought instant joy. Tires on pavement, a roaring engine, our big yellow bus coming through the white sea to carry us away. It got louder as it steadily came closer. Then there they were, faint headlights heading right toward us.

They say that light travels faster than the speed of sound, but even at five years old, I would have argued that I could hear the bus before I could see its headlights. Perhaps it was because the fog covered the light in the darkness.

Then, the best sound of all, brakes screeching to a halt, followed by air forced through metal. Then when the doors opened, a sound that said, "Welcome aboard."

My brother and I scrambled from our post. We stood at the bottom of the steps for a second, staring up at the tall king of a driver with his light gray hair who looked down from his giant green throne.

He grinned. "Good morning! They should have delayed the buses with the fog being so thick this morning, but I made it."

For that, we were thankful! In that instance our big smiles told our bus driver, Mr. Beasley, he was our most favorite person on Earth. He was our rescuer, our savior, the one who had come to find us trapped in the fog.

Since ours was his first stop of the morning, the bus was totally empty. We could choose any seat that we wanted to claim as our own for the whole ride to school. Most days that was an amazing feat, but on that day, it was only a small victory in the scheme of things. On cold, foggy mornings like this, being inside the big metal school bus felt like being trapped inside an ice cube. The only solace was the middle seats where the heaters were. My big brother and I walked down the aisle, passing by several of the short green leather seats.

Mr. Beasley hollered for us to, "Find the heat!"

That we did. My brother found the middle seat on the right with the space heater on the floor. I found the one on the left. Those particular seats didn't have as much leg room because the heater created a big bump that you had to rest your feet on. A small sacrifice to pay for the price of being a bit warmer.

The heaters were blowing warm air full blast, but on that giant bus, we could only feel it if we were right next to the vent where it was coming from. So, I gathered up my whole tiny five-year-old self and sat on the floor, resting between the cold, green leather seat, and the heater. I was as close to the heat as I could possibly get without getting burned.

Whoever got on the bus next wasn't going to stand a chance of taking any of *my* heat. My brother looked over at me and laughed as he huddled as close as he could to *his* heater, where he would stay for most of the ride into town. For us, it was just a normal start to the morning to travel from our ranch to the tiny town where we went to school.

I was thankful that I didn't have to make the journey alone because we both knew there would be days when I would be going without my big brother. Neither of us knew what those days would be like, and we didn't bother preparing for them. We were just two kids who lived for the moment and embraced each one as they came to us.

KINDERGARTEN

~KIMBERLEY'S THOUGHT~

THE BUS HAD BECOME NOISY and crowded as it carried us closer to town. I pulled myself up from my spot by the heater. I looked across the aisle at my brother, with his balding blonde head, chatting away with his friends. Almost every seat was full of kids anxious to start their school day.

I climbed up onto my seat and looked out the window. The fog had lifted just enough for me to see the old two-story white house. Whenever I saw it, I was reminded of one of my mom's favorite poems by Joyce Kilmer, "The House With Nobody In It." That's what she called the white house. I always had mixed emotions when I looked at that sturdy-built old place just outside of town. I imagined what it must have looked like when it was first built, with a happy family living inside of it.

Then I waited patiently to spot the Candy Cane house soon coming up ahead.

At the edge of town was the Pink Store. I know it had another name, but to me it was the Pink Store, one of two grocery stores in our tiny town of Livingston. We would usually buy our groceries at Serv-All, the other grocery store in the middle of town, but we occasionally bought a few things at the Pink Store. I don't remember what we bought there. I spent all of my time trying to step on the big, pink, black, and white squares on the floor. I imagined them being part of a fancy checkerboard of some sort. My brother and I would challenge each other to jump from one square of the same color to the other without stepping on one of the numerous white squares.

He usually always beat me at that game too.

Through the window on the other side of the street, I could see the giant high school that looked like a castle. I imagined it had been built by kings, and that my mom, aunts, grandparents, and other relatives walked through those big arches. I wondered what it would be like when I went to school there. I didn't know at the time that I would never get to call that amazing-looking building *my* high school, but how was I to know? I was too young to realize that we never know what the future holds.

I was suddenly jolted back to reality when something red caught my eye. The house I had been patiently waiting to see.

There it was…the Candy Cane House.

Wedged between two other houses on Main Street, it was painted white with red trim. It had a white metal fence in front that kept its little yard protected from the outside world. Sometimes large white candy canes with red stripes were hanging from it. No matter the time of year, though, the house always looked the same, like a giant candy cane. I don't know who lived in it, but I imagined that they really loved Christmas. Seeing their house always brought a big smile to my face and happiness in my heart. After all, who didn't love Christmas?

Next, we passed by the park. We loved to slide down the tall metal slide, and when our dad had practice at the baseball field, we played in the dirt with our little cars. But when Dad was playing in a game, we watched him instead of playing on the playground equipment.

Dad was so much fun to watch! I couldn't see the baseball field very well on this foggy day, but I knew it was there. I pictured my dad hitting the ball into the outfield and running the bases as fast as he could. After the games were over, my big brother and I would run around them too, just like Dad. Our mom and dad loved baseball! They loved watching, playing, keeping score, and coaching. Later in life, I would learn that my dad had been asked to play professional baseball. It was a story that always made him a little sad because that dream never saw reality.

When my dad told the professional baseball story, it always led to another one that brought sadness to his heart. It was about his days playing football in high school and college. Dad wasn't very tall, but he could run really fast. He was a star running back on his San Francisco Abraham Lincoln High School football team, until he was shot in the arm by a good friend during a bird hunting trip. For many years after that, pieces of birdshot made their way out of his arm. However, he had healed enough to return to football the following season. A year after recovering from Dad's traumatic injury, his own father died unexpectedly from stomach cancer. My dad was just sixteen years old, and his world had been turned completely upside down.

A raging alcoholic, his mom was so distraught she had to be committed to a mental hospital. His brother, who was eleven years older than him, was busy raising a family of his own. Football and baseball were my dad's way of escaping the realities of the world when it came crashing down around him. He put his heart and soul into every game he played and later went on to play college football after graduating from high school.

As the bus drew closer to the school, I could see kids walking and riding their bikes. I wondered what that might be like, to live close enough to the school that walking each morning was an option. A part of me was jealous of my friends who lived in town, whereas another part of me was thankful to be toasty and warm inside the yellow bus. With that, I blew a big breath on the window. When it fogged up, I drew a little heart with my finger right in the center of the condensation.

Cold, winter mornings had their own special kind of joy.

When the bus came to a stop in front of Campus Park Elementary School, a bunch of us scrambled single file to the exit. I was the tiniest, but one of the most noticeable with my bright green hazel-colored eyes and long blonde hair. I squeezed into the line near my friends, who all had brown or black hair.

I guess my brother spotted me in an instant because he hollered, "Have a good day!"

I knew he was watching me closely as I walked off the bus and headed to the kindergarten playground. Clint always did that; then he stayed on the bus to the next stop. The school where the big kids went. It was just for fourth through eighth grades, but to me, anyone who was older than a third grader was a *big kid*.

I headed straight for the huge, silver, heavy, metal teeter-totters to play with my friends. It was still a bit foggy, so I couldn't see all of them, but I knew they were there somewhere. Many of them were probably playing tag in the fog on the grassy area away from the playground equipment. That was always a lot of fun on days like this because it was a mix of tag and hide-and-go-seek. It was easy to hide in the low-hanging clouds that hovered over the playground. A few other friends were probably taking turns going down the tall silver slide. I thought about possibly playing tag in the fog, or going down the slide, but stayed with my decision of spending at least a few minutes on my favorite piece of equipment, the teeter-totters.

When one of my classmates was on the other end, since I was so tiny, I would sail high, almost to the sky. Then that person would jump up to bring me back down to Earth. Back and forth we went, losing all track of time, until our teacher rang the metal triangle for us to line up for class.

I was a bit sad that play time was over, but happy to go inside where it was warmer. I quickly jumped off the cold, metal teeter-totter and got in line right outside my classroom door. I huddled close to my friends; school was one of my most favorite places to be. Here, I could escape from the realities of real life and soak in every minute of fun with my classmates. My friends and I would spend as much time as we could talking, reading stories, learning new things, and playing make-believe. It was in those moments that everything in the world was perfect.

It was also the place where the teachers inspired me to do my best and to work hard. The teachers in my early years of school were the ones who put me on the path to becoming a teacher myself one day.

School wasn't all fine and dandy, though. Kindergarten certainly had its drawbacks. One of the biggest; the dreaded nap time. After lunch, all of us kids were instructed to lie on blue plastic mats to take a nap while soothing music came from the record player. The tunes were nice, and the mats were comfortable enough, but taking a nap at school was the last thing on Earth that I wanted to do!

I went to school to have fun with my friends and teachers, which was not allowed during nap time. While we rested, the teachers talked quietly among themselves. I covered my head with my jacket and pretended like I was camping in my own personal little tent. I told myself stories in my head, about fishing trips, or living in a huge castle, and riding on a horse through the forest. You know—the usual kid fantasy stuff. It never helped me fall asleep, but it did make the boring nap time go by faster.

Suddenly the line started to move, I followed my friends into the classroom, and we each took off our coats and hung them on the hooks by the door. Thankfully, the uneventful nap time wouldn't take place until after lunch. It would be a few hours before I'd have to prepare for resting on the dreaded blue mat. The next few hours went by quickly; we read books, played in the pretend kitchen, practiced counting using buttons and bottle caps, made crafts out of paper, and ate paste—even though we were repeatedly told not to. After a busy morning of playing, talking, and learning, it was time for lunch. A favorite for most of my friends, but not me.

I found it impossible to talk and chew my food at the same time, so I was always the last one sitting at the lunch table, trying to finish whatever I could while my friends went to the playground. There were a few days here and there, though, when my stomach growled enough that food was more the priority than talking. It was those times that I wasn't the last kid sitting at the lunch table while the ladies cleaned up. One might think that would help me to learn how to eat fast, but those days were few and far between. I ate quickly only on special occasions; when I was especially hungry or when the food was extraordinarily good.

On that cold, fall day, the aroma of green beans and chicken gravy hovered in the air. I knew in an instant that this was going to be one of those special occasion days. It all smelled so good that I could almost taste it. My stomach started growling just at the thought of how delicious the chicken swimming in gravy would taste over warm mashed potatoes. Before the lunch ladies could scoop the deliciousness onto our trays, though, we would need to hand our lunch cards to the lunch card lady.

She sat at a little wooden table right next to the kitchen

entrance. She was an older lady with curly gray hair and big gold wire-rimmed glasses that rested on her nose. I didn't know her name, but she clearly knew mine. She hole-punched our pink or blue lunch cards every day. They were used to keep track of who paid or didn't pay; the pink cards were for free or reduced lunch, and the blue cards were for paid lunch. My card was always pink. That meant that we were on government assistance for our meals, but I didn't know this until a friend pointed it out a few years later.

Every time the lunch card lady saw me, she always asked me how my big brother was doing. I always smiled a big smile and said, "Fine," so I could quickly move on and get to where the food was. After all, I needed all the time I could get to eat my lunch so I could go out and play. I never knew how to answer her question when she asked how my brother was doing. I mean, why didn't she just ask him how he was doing? And why didn't she ever ask me how *I* was doing? *Nobody* ever asked me how I was doing. But it was okay. After all, I was fine, but it did intrigue me that everyone was always so curious about my brother. Looking back now, I know that the lunch card lady meant well, but at five years old, I felt like she was asking me a question that I couldn't possibly know the answer to.

On this day, though, my big brother really wasn't *fine*, and I knew that. Our parents always found it best to be truthful instead of sheltering us from the realities of life. My brother was *fine* to me, but to the rest of the world, my parents included, he had leukemia, he was the boy dying of cancer. I knew that this was a day that I could actually give the lunch card lady an answer other than *fine*, and in a strange way, I was kind of excited. So, as I patiently waited in line to give her my pink card, I prepared by playing the anticipated conversation over in my mind.

Finally, I handed her my lunch card, and as expected, she asked me the usual question.

"How is your brother doing?"

I smiled my big kindergarten missing teeth smile and gave her the answer that I had rehearsed in my head. I used my powerful big girl voice to tell her all that I knew.

"He relapsed, for the second time, and he has testicular cancer now, too. Today is the last day that he'll be in school for a while because he'll be starting treatments again. He'll be taking some new medicines too."

The lunch card lady shrugged her shoulders at me and said, "I knew that. I just meant, how is he?"

Well, that didn't go as expected. What exactly was it she wanted to know? To me, he seemed *fine*. After all, he had just beaten me at the dirt Indian Bowl game for the hundredth time, and he was at school today. What was I supposed to tell her? I had prepared myself for a much different response. I wasn't sure what she would say, but it wasn't what I thought it would be. I'd seen other adults respond to my parents with some gushing, "I'm so sorry," or "Everything will be okay." But not the lunch card lady. I guess she wanted to know something that I didn't know how to answer.

So, with that, I looked away from her and quickly moved along. From that day on, when anyone ever asked how my brother was doing, I usually always went back to my safe answer of, *fine*.

Sometimes explaining things to adults was really hard.

I tried to brush the conversation off as I watched the lunch ladies pouring scoops of green beans, mashed potatoes, and bits of shredded chicken swimming in golden colored gravy onto our lunch trays. The lunch ladies, or cooks, as some of my friends called them, always seemed so happy to see us kindergarteners as we walked past each of their stations. They watched us closely, I guess to ensure that none of us dropped our big, heavy plastic trays.

They were various colors of light blue, lime green, soft speckled pink, and a rusty yellow. I always secretly hoped for a pink tray.

For some reason, the food always looked prettier on that color. Some of my friends brought lunch from home, so they didn't carry a tray. Instead, they were assigned a table where they could enjoy their special homemade treats while the rest of us walked through the lunch line. Most days, we would watch in awe, wondering what special treasures they had inside their brown paper sacks. But on this day, I was happy as a clam to be eating this delicious meal.

I quickly sat down to eat before my talking took over the task of chewing. With each bite, I replayed the lunch card lady conversation over in my head. I tried hard to make sense of it all. It felt as if she knew something I didn't. There was something hidden in her eyes and mixed up in her words.

This day of kindergarten hadn't turned out quite like the others. Something felt strange and off. I could hardly wait to get home so that I could talk about it with my family. I was hopeful that they could help explain the lunch card lady conversation with me in a way that I could understand.

HOME ON THE RANCH

THE REST OF THE SCHOOL DAY flew by, and before I knew it, I could see Mimi and Bompa, my great-grandparents', white house with green trim. My grandparents' house was next door with big pine and persimmon trees in their front yard, and three mailboxes lined up on the edge of the street. All of that told me I was home.

The big yellow school bus slowly came to a stop in front of the ranch. Mr. Beasley got off and stood in the middle of the street to stop any traffic that might happen to be traveling down that desolate country road, and he ensured that I made it to my destination safely. I smiled and waved goodbye to him as I skipped across the street and up the dirt driveway toward our house. I was home a few hours before my brother because, as a kindergartner, I only went to school for half a day. Mr. Beasley, or another bus driver, would be dropping Clint off later.

We lived in a yellow and white double-wide mobile home on what our family always referred to as, "The Ranch." It was one hundred and twenty acres of grapevines nestled in the California

Central Valley. Many of the grape rows had walnut trees at the ends. The majority of the grapes were harvested each fall and sold to a nearby winery. My grandparents' grapes were then turned into fine wine and labeled as "Estate Cellars." A different variety of grapes on the ranch was picked by hand and laid on paper trays to become raisins. They were then boxed and sold to *Sun-Maid.* The last of the grapes were then harvested for us to eat or to turn into juice.

The Ranch had been in our family since the late 1800s. It was first started by a company out of San Francisco as a test ranch for a variety of crops to see what would grow best in the prime Central Valley soil, and where the weather conditions were ideal for many crops. The test consisted of walnuts, almonds, plums, figs, grapes, and a variety of other produce.

My great-grandparents were keepers of the ranch and eventually purchased it as their own in the early 1900s. Grapes took over as the predominant crop and eventually became the sole income producer of the land. By the time I came into the picture, a few trees remained. One plum, one fig, one pomegranate, two persimmon, several walnut, a few shade trees, and over a hundred acres of grapes. Come harvest time there was always plenty for us to eat from our own land.

That was something I totally took for granted until much later in life, when grabbing a pomegranate off the tree was no longer a possibility. I realized just how blessed I had been; the ranch was a child's dream of endless adventure. It was a place where I could play outside for hours upon hours without ever running out of things to do.

I ran up the driveway between my great-grandparents' and my grandparents' houses. It didn't take long before my grandma greeted me.

"Hi, Kimmy!" She was standing on her and my grandpa's back

porch waiting for me. Her big brown curls outlined the smile on her face.

To get to her, I ran past the old swing set and between the two old rusty metal wagon wheels nestled at the end of their sidewalk. She was wearing her usual black slacks with a contrasting short-sleeve red polyester blouse. She held the wood-framed screen door open for me, and I ran inside their little yellow farmhouse. She quickly closed both the screen and wooden doors behind me.

When my grandparents were married, they purchased two Japanese Internment Camp houses that were used during WWII and had them moved to The Ranch. They put them together to create one house. It was a story I heard many times in my life, and I would often look for the seam in the ceiling where the two houses were joined.

I was quickly reminded that I was in a place of comfort. The smell of coffee, dust, propane, burning firewood, and butterscotch candy filled me with calm. Grandma helped me climb up on one of the black barstools at the wooden breakfast bar. It was built by a family friend and had been there since before I was born. It had a smooth black top, and on the front a carved big letter *P* that represented my grandparents' last name. Everyone gathered there to talk, drink, and eat snacks.

I began chattering to her about my day, and Grandma handed me a shiny red apple and a small glass of 7-Up. I talked first about which boy I liked that week. She always had a way of making me fess up about my newest crush. Even at five, I was pretty boy crazy. Grandma scrunched up her nose and said, "Oh him, he's so cute."

I blushed and continued talking. She grabbed an apple too and taught me how to twist the stem around while saying the letters of the alphabet with each twist. She told me that whatever letter I was on when the stem came off was the first initial of the name of a boy who liked me. I laughed at that silly thought and twisted and twisted until the stem came off. While I took big bites out of the small red apple, we listed every boy's name that we could think of that started with that letter. Thinking about a boy liking me made me giggle with embarrassment.

I brought up the lunch lady incident. Grandma listened to my story with anticipation as well as with tears forming in her eyes. She squeezed my hand and said, "You answered that lady's question right, Kimmy, your brother did relapse, and you're also right that Clint is fine. We're all just fine."

I knew that *fine* didn't necessarily mean that my brother's cancer was going to go away. I also knew that bad things were still happening in our family, but her agreeing with my answer made it all feel a little better. My grandma had a way of believing that all was right with the world, even when it wasn't. I still didn't quite understand the conversation with the lunch lady, but instantly, my day felt bright again.

Shortly after that, Papa walked into the house. For most of our lives we kids called our grandpa, Papa, but everyone else called him Jerry. He came in for a little break from a busy day of ranch work and jokingly said, "Who's this dumb little kid sitting at my bar?"

We all laughed as he took off his heavy coat and put his fur-lined winter hat on the old pencil sharpener that was hanging on the wall by the door. He then turned to look at my grandma with his brown balding head and light brown eyes. "How now, brown cow?"

She chuckled and kissed him hello. I watched in wonder, not quite understanding why what he said was so funny, but it was.

Dad followed quickly behind my grandpa. He came in their house wearing his heavy red, white, and blue coat with a matching red, blue, and yellow ski hat. Even though the fog had mostly lifted, it was still cloudy and cold; enough that anyone should have been bundled up if they were going to spend any length of time outside.

He glanced over my way, his blue eyes shining brightly. "Hi, Kimmers!"

I was so happy to see him, and I smiled my biggest smile! His hello was welcoming, but it was also a cue that it was time for me to finish my snack and move along.

I quickly finished eating my apple and drank all my 7-Up so that I could go outside and help my dad with the rest of the day's ranch work. There was always lots to do, and I knew Dad would enjoy my company. He loved teaching me about each chore and patiently showed me how to do many of them alongside him. I couldn't wait to see what was in store for the next few hours, then at the end of the work day, I would see my brothers and Mom.

She was still busy at work. Mom loved her job as a teacher's aide at the school that Clint went to. After Mom got off work, she'd pick up my little brother from the babysitter before coming home. She usually made it shortly after the bus dropped Clint off from school. The whole family would be united for supper, when we all looked forward to spending time together.

WORKING
"DOWN THE FIELD"

MY DAD HELD MY HAND as we walked together in the dirt from my grandparents' house. Before reaching our place, my dad took a little side stop at the Quonset hut. We went inside the huge silver metal building to gather some tools. My mom told me that the hut was once used as a mechanic shop before it was moved to the ranch. My great-grandpa bought it to use as his own shop. The grape harvester was kept there most of the year. It is also where they worked on tractors, the tools were organized, and old family heirlooms were stored. For the most part, it was a wide-open space with a cement floor, metal walls, a few old broken windows, and a rounded metal roof.

At harvest time, when the harvester was kept outside and the tractors were hard at work, I would imagine that the Quonset was my own personal skating rink. The wide-open space made a perfect roller rink. I would skate in there for hours while I pretended that a crowd of people cheered me on as I twirled around, skated backwards, and jumped in the air. I was certain that I would be a professional skater one day. But after we moved off the ranch, I seldom roller-skated.

Far in the back of the Quonset was a set of old wooden stairs that led to a small loft where, among other things, some of my mom's baby toys were kept. We kids weren't allowed up there because it was too dangerous, but every now and then my brother would talk me into sneaking up with him to look at the hidden treasures. We would sit on my mom's old rubber rocking horse and admire my great-great-grandma's old rocking chair. We were told the closed dusty boxes were filled with special antiques. It really wasn't safe for us to be up in the loft area. There were holes in the wooden floorboards and black widow spiders everywhere, but I always felt that my brother would protect me from those dangers.

While Dad gathered up a hammer, nails, and a few other things from the workbench, I played with the old metal vise that sat on a stand close to the wall of the Quonset.

"Be careful not to smash your fingers in that vise," Dad reminded me.

"I know. I won't." I slowly pushed the oval-shaped metal handle of the vise up into the hole that it rested in and watched it slam into the end. The metal ball stopped it from going all the way through the hole. I moved it carefully as in the past I'd gotten a blood blister from pushing it through the hole too quickly.

Dad and I walked side by side to the red Massey Ferguson tractor and wooden trailer that was parked just outside. We would be working from the tractor and trailer for the next few hours. Dad put the tools onto the short redwood flatbed trailer, then we walked the rest of the way to our house.

When we got to our big white front porch, we were greeted by mama cat, a calico mix, a few of her kittens, and our dogs, Ringo,

Banjo, and Ranger. Ringo and Banjo were strays that someone dropped off near our mailbox over the summer. It wasn't uncommon for people to abandon their pet dogs and cats out in the country. They could find water at our place, so many of the strays eventually ended up there.

Ringo and Banjo were just puppies when my grandpa found them tied up in burlap sacks. Ringo was a mutt who had short black hair with brown streaks on his face and legs. Many said that he was a mix of Rottweiler and black lab. Banjo may have been Ringo's brother, but other than their size, they didn't look anything alike. They both had grown tall enough that I could pet them without having to lean down at all.

With short light-brown hair, Ringo had a solid black stripe down his back. For the first week or so that we had him, we spent hours trying to wash the black stripe off his back, thinking that it was oil, but it wouldn't come off. Finally, a friend told us that Banjo was a Rhodesian ridgeback, a lion-hunting dog. I wasn't sure if that was true or not, though, because he didn't seem mean enough to hunt lions. But nonetheless, our friend was probably right.

Ranger was our oldest dog. He was born many years before I was. I don't know exactly when, but I remember him being much older than me. He was my parents' first baby and was our mighty protector. A big German shepherd husky mix, he would let us pull his tail and ride on his back for hours on end, at the same time he was on guard to protect us from whatever dangers might lurk our way. He was the sweetest dog in the world and would have gone to the ends of the Earth to keep us safe. I was told that he could be mean to strangers, but I never saw it.

I gave him a big hug and patted him on the head to say, "Hello," then walked into our house.

My dad and I walked through the sliding glass door of our mobile home. To the left we passed by the large 1970s Sony record player high up on a wooden stand. Below were shelves of record albums. My dad's yellow turnout gear from the fire department was on the floor to our right. He was a volunteer for the Livingston Volunteer Fire Department, so he always had his gear ready close by the door for the moments that his red fire pager went off, and he had to respond quickly. Next to his turnout gear was a large wooden amplifier box where Dad could plug in one of his guitars.

Our home was welcoming and filled with all my favorite things. Shiny wood paneling made our house feel more like a cabin instead of a mobile home. Its walls embraced everyone, and the plush dark green and gold carpet cushioned our feet.

Our house might have felt small to some, but to me it was a mansion. It had three bedrooms, two bathrooms, a big yellow and white kitchen, a living room large enough for us to play touch football in, and a dining room—it wouldn't acquire a table until a few years later. The family room, where all the adults always seemed to gather, opened up to the kitchen.

In the center of the family room was the large wooden pool table with a green felt top. A large glass light adorned with shades of green, white, red, yellow, and the words Pool Room, hung over the table, inviting everyone to play. The pool cues, balls, and chalk hung on the wall to the east of the table. Three large open cutouts in the shared wall with the living room made the house feel much larger than it actually was.

The wall to the west of the pool table was covered with wooden shelves and filled with Mom's books. After years of begging for a library of her own, my dad built the shelves for her with 2x6s and black shelf brackets. She loved having a place to store all of her books and read them whenever she got the chance.

My dad had put together a small silver model airplane and a red model fire truck. He placed them in the few empty areas of the bookshelves. I always wondered about the ship in a bottle in the middle of the top shelf. How in the world did that ship get inside that bottle?

A small wooden bar filled with a few glasses, alcohol, and some fun little bar games adorned the back wall, closest to the large window. On top of the bar sat a couple of glass bobblehead dolls that my dad had acquired from Giants baseball and 49er football games over the years. On the wall behind the bar were lamps from several different brands. My favorite was the one that said "Olympia" at the top. When it was turned on, that lamp on it looked as if a waterfall was cascading from it. I would stare at its bright blue and white colors, wondering where I could find something so beautiful in real life.

On the same wall as the record player was my dad's pride and joy, his old 1960s guitar. He would spend any free time that he had playing records, humming tunes, and strumming his guitar for all to hear. He tried many times to teach my mom, brothers, and me how to play it, but none of us had the patience for it like he did. Besides, I just wanted to listen to him play it. No matter what I was doing, or where I was in the house, it brought such calmness to my heart to hear him strum each chord. Even at times when he thought he wasn't playing a certain tune quite right, I always thought it sounded perfect.

Dad set his gloves on the pool table, and I ran into my bedroom to change out of my school clothes and into my play clothes; Mom called them that because they weren't quite good enough to wear out in public because of stains, or holes, but certainly were good enough to work and play in at home. I quickly put on my blue jeans with holes, a Dallas Cowboys sweatshirt that was once Clint's, and warm socks.

After I changed, I ran through the living room to find my dad in the kitchen. His almost shoulder-length brown hair trailed out of the back of his ski hat as he stood at the breakfast bar refilling his tall green and silver Stanley thermos with hot chocolate. He screwed the top on tight and walked back over to the pool table to grab his gloves. Before we went back outside, he made sure my shoes were tied, my jacket was zipped up tight, my ski cap was on, and my gloves fit my hands snuggly.

He looked right at me. "You ready to go to work?"

I grinned. "Yep!"

I ran out the sliding glass door to the red tractor and waited for my dad to climb aboard. He set his thermos in its plastic cup holder on the inside edge of the tractor, then grabbed me up and sat me on the tractor seat. I climbed from there to the wheel well of the tractor to hold on tight. Dad sat down and turned the tractor key until the engine came to life with its low rumbling, putt, putt, bang. He helped me climb back down from my perch on the wheel well to his lap. I then helped him steer the tractor down the field, turning the big wheel the best I could.

That day was for fixing wooden posts and wires. We drove the tractor between the grapevines looking for wooden posts that needed to be straightened or replaced in the soft country dirt. We also looked for wires that were coming loose, they would need to be re-stretched and re-nailed to secure them so that the grapevines would stay wrapped in their proper places.

We drove a little way until we found a post that needed fixing. Dad stopped the tractor, we both climbed down and walked to the trailer. I grabbed the hammer, and Dad picked up the nails that looked like little *U*'s. I tried my best to hold the wooden post in place while he hammered away, fixing the loose wires. I climbed up onto the trailer where I sat while my dad drove the tractor to the next fixing spot. We worked for the next few hours searching for leaning or broken posts, stretching wire, hammering U-shaped nails, taking breaks, and drinking hot chocolate to warm us up.

The whole time we worked, Dad would tell me the names of

each tool that we were using and showed me how to properly use them. Some of the tools were too heavy for my little arms to lift, but it didn't stop me from trying. He also told me stories about how he fixed fences and other things at the places he'd worked when he was a park ranger. He loved being a park ranger, and I'm sure he had never dreamed of quitting that job. It involved working with his hands as well as talking to and helping people. Two things that he really loved doing.

Before I was born, my dad worked hard as a park ranger and was always thankful that he'd reached his goal of becoming one. A few years after he and Mom were married, they settled in the foothills of Del Puerto Canyon, California; his first placement was at the state park there. A few years after my big brother was born, Dad was transferred to a different California state park. It was there in the old gold mining town of La Grange, where I was born. My parents loved living in La Grange and probably would have lived there for many more years if life hadn't changed their plans.

It was also in that little old mining town where my brother was diagnosed with cancer. Stage 4 Leukemia; a blood cancer that was seen by most everyone at that time as a death sentence. He was only four years old when he was diagnosed, just five months before I was born. My mom almost lost me due to the stress of his diagnosis and had to be bedridden for a short time to ensure that she didn't miscarry. It was later decided that I was too strong and determined, or too stubborn, to be miscarried, and she brought me into this world with no problems at all.

My parents tried hard to keep on living the life they'd dreamed of having, where my dad would continue to be a park ranger in the foothills. However, the journey back and forth from home to the children's hospital, over three hours one way, became cumbersome, and life presented a difficult decision for them to make. Because of the cost of medical bills and travel, they had no choice but to move onto my great-grandparents' ranch in the Central Valley, where my mom was born and raised. Moving onto the ranch meant that Dad would have to give up the job he loved as a park ranger.

Giving up a dream job and life is not a decision that anyone wants to make, but my parents tried to focus on the positive. They were thankful that with the help of my grandparents, they were able to purchase their own, first-ever home. It was a double-wide mobile home that was moved onto my great-grandparents' property. The house was situated just a few feet from my grandparents' house, which would allow them, when needed, to help with us kids.

Moving onto the ranch was a path in my parents' life they hadn't planned for. One of those unexpected twists that takes one down a new path. It was a selfless decision that they made from their love for their children and their love for each other. A decision that changed the course of their history. Even though I had spent the first few years of my life living near a cemetery in the foothills, life on the ranch is the only childhood I ever knew.

Dad and I were almost done working for the day, and my stomach told me that it was getting close to supper time. I was having fun with Dad, but I was eager to get home to eat and see my mom and brothers.

I patiently watched my dad stretch the grapevine wire. "How much longer before we're done for today?"

"This is the last post for the day, Pumpkin." My dad always had lots of silly nicknames for me, and Pumpkin was one of his favorites.

I laughed. "I'm not a pumpkin."

He smiled. "I know, but you're as cute as one."

I giggled and hurriedly climbed up onto the trailer.

In my rush, I got a big splinter in my index finger. I tried hard not to cry, but it really hurt. After Dad finished stretching the wire and securing all the tools in the toolbox, he noticed that I was picking at my finger, and that I had tears rolling down my cheeks.

He stopped for a second and looked at me. "What's wrong?"

I held up my finger so he could take a closer look.

He shook his head. "This one is too deep for me to get it out with my fingernails. It will have to wait until we get home."

"It really hurts." I was a little confused because I'd had many splinters in my life.

Dad explained, "The reason it hurts worse than other splinters is because this trailer is made of redwood."

A view of the Quonset hut on our ranch and the neighbor's almond trees in the background as Papa took Cody and me for a ride on his 3-wheeler.

I pondered his statement as I sat there. I'm not sure if redwood splinters really hurt worse than other types, but for some reason, his justification of my pain made me feel better.

Dad helped me climb off the trailer and onto the tractor. I climbed up on the wheel well until he sat down in the tractor seat, then he picked me up and sat me on his lap. I held my finger as he drove back to the house.

As it got colder I could see my breath, and the sun was starting to set, calling an end to a busy day of school and work. When Dad parked the tractor and trailer at the end of the Quonset hut, the air smelled of a savory blend of tomatoes, onions, and garlic, telling me that something delicious was being cooked at home. My dad grabbed his big thermos and helped me climb down from the tractor. I still held tightly to my splinter finger.

Dad checked over the equipment as I ran ahead of him to the house in hopes that supper would soon be ready. The thought of getting my splinter removed and eating dinner gave me an extra spring in my step.

SUPPER TIME

As I ran through the sliding glass door and into the house, my legs were quickly pulled out from under me by my big brother, who had been hiding under the pool table just waiting to attack. He threw me to the ground and tickled me until I caught my breath just long enough to holler, "Mercy!"

Clint sat on my legs and held both of my arms down. He laughed. "Are you sure you're ready to give up?"

Mom yelled out from the kitchen, "Knock it off before someone gets hurt!"

Not wanting to get in trouble, Clint and I quickly jumped up and ran into the kitchen together.

The surprise attack from my brother made me forget about the pain in my finger for a few minutes, but as soon as I reached my mom, my finger throbbed with pain once again. I showed her the splinter like it was a battle wound that I'd acquired in a long-forgotten war. She quietly left the kitchen and returned with tweezers, a needle, and the dreaded red bottle of antiseptic spray to doctor me up. I referred to the bottle of antiseptic as *red burn spray* because it burned awful when it was sprayed on my skin. Seeing that red glass bottle instantly brought tears to my eyes because I knew it was going to hurt worse than the splinter ever did. I later learned its real name was Mercurochrome.

I hid my finger behind my back. "It's okay, just let the splinter be." I'd live with the splinter in my finger for the rest of my life to avoid having it sprayed with that demon red burning spray!

Mom laughed. "If I don't take that splinter out, your finger could get infected. If that happens, then you might have to have your finger amputated, cut off to stop the infection."

Cut off? This brought on more tears as I cautiously let her take my little finger into her soft hands. She worked quickly, and the splinter was out before I could even count to five. Remarkably, the pain was instantly gone.

She sighed. "That was a big splinter. I bet the reason it hurt so bad was that it was a redwood splinter."

What did my mom and dad have against redwood? They must have had redwood splinters of their own before because they both had talked about them as if they were experts on the matter. Mom then sprayed my finger with the dreaded burn spray before I had time to stop her.

"Ouch!" I hollered with agony.

Clint watched intently, probably thankful that he didn't have a splinter in his own finger.

Mom's long brown hair swayed back and forth as she washed her hands at the kitchen sink. She put the first-aid stuff aside and gave Clint and me an uncooked spaghetti noodle to chomp on while she finished cooking supper. We quietly watched her work until we had finished eating our noodles.

"You two go and wash up for supper, then come back and set the table," she instructed.

The *table* was actually a breakfast bar that was connected to the kitchen counter just off the stove. It had a light brown, glassy wood laminate finish and was just big enough for Mom, Dad, Clint, and me to sit at comfortably. Underneath it was a little cubby hole that made for the perfect hiding spot when we would play hide-and-go-seek.

Clint ran ahead of me to ensure that he washed his hands before I did. He always had to be first at everything. He seemed to think that being the first one to wash his hands before supper somehow made him a champion of some sort; of hand washing, I suppose. I would sometimes try to outrun him in hopes of getting to the sink before he did, but I usually tripped and fell in the process, so it was just easier to let him win. Besides, I didn't mind at all letting him get into the bathroom to wash his hands before me because I needed to make a side stop first.

My little brother was lying on the floor all snuggled up on his favorite blanket. Cody was the cutest little boy that I'd ever seen, and I would have easily spent hours just staring at him if I could. I stood over him with so much pride, thinking how I was the luckiest sister in the world to have such an adorable little brother whose light blond hair was just starting to grow. I would have paraded him through the streets for the whole world to see if my parents would have let me. But, at that point in my life, I was lucky enough to just sit with him on my lap for a few minutes before I had to give him to a grown-up. Even though he had just turned a year old, I still didn't quite understand that he wasn't just mine, and that I had to share him with others. I did understand, though, that I wasn't big enough or fast enough to watch him all by myself. He was the fastest-moving one-year-old anyone had ever seen. When Cody was awake, he was the brightest light in our house. His spunk and joy made it impossible for anyone to be sad for even a second around him.

I watched him sleep with so many questions in my mind. When would he wake up? When would he be old enough to really play with me? Would he ride the bus to school with me one day? I thought about how I had so badly wanted him to be a girl.

The day that Cody was born, Clint and I were at our grandparents' house. We anxiously waited for the phone to ring, and they were asking us if we wanted a new baby brother or sister. Clint and I debated back and forth for a while on which would be better. He wanted a brother since he already had a sister, but I really wanted a sister because I already had a brother.

Finally, we heard the phone ring, and I saw the vibration of the old black rotary phone that was sitting on the end table at the edge of the couch. My grandma jumped up to answer it. She talked quietly for a few minutes to whoever was on the other end as we scrunched up next to her on the couch, trying to hear who she was talking to. The conversation was short, so she quickly hung up the receiver and turned to us.

"Okay, you both wanted a sister, right?"

Clint hollered out, "Awe *man!*"

I was a bit confused because she had a twinkle in her eye that told me she had more to say, but I hollered anyway, "Yay!"

My grandma scrunched up her nose and laughed. "Well, you didn't get a sister, you have a baby brother."

"I knew it, I knew it! I knew it was going to be a boy!" Clint sang and danced around.

Tears started to form in my little eyes. I had so wanted a sister.

And even more than that, I wanted to win at something. For some reason, I thought that if my mom had a girl then I would have won the debate of which was better to have, a sister instead of another brother. Instead, I lost. Clint had won. *Again*. His dream of having a little brother came true.

My grandma took me into her arms and squeezed me close. "Oh, Kimmy, it's okay. All that matters is that your mom is fine and that the baby is healthy. You are a sister now with both a big brother and a little brother, and that's really special."

A warmth came over me, and my sadness quickly turned to joy because she was right. A part of me felt so bad for not just thinking about the fact that the baby and my mom were healthy, because that was the most important thing of all.

"Do you want to go and see him?" Grandma asked both Clint and me.

At the same time, Clint and I shouted out, "We get to go and see him?"

"Yep, go get in the car."

We hurried outside and ran to get in their green 1970s Ford Galaxie. The next thing I remember is that we were at the hospital putting on special gowns and masks before we were taken into a room where Mom, Dad, and our new baby brother were. The moment I saw him with his huge brown eyes, soft white skin, and tiny hands, I forgot all about the brother/sister debate. I was totally and completely in love with *this* baby. *My* new little brother.

My thoughts about the day my baby brother was born were soon interrupted by Clint's booming voice.

"Go and wash your hands!" Clint hollered as he walked passed me. "I washed mine before you." He proudly reminded me.

Suddenly remembering how hungry I was, I hurried along to the bathroom.

Dad was in the house now and washed up for supper while Mom finished cooking. Clint and I scooted brown barstools from the family room to the breakfast bar, ensuring there was one for each of us. Clint then pushed the high chair over close, making sure that it was still sitting on the linoleum part so that when Cody threw his food on the floor, it wouldn't get all over the green carpet.

Next, Clint and I set the *table* with plates, forks, paper towels, and glasses. After we thought it looked good enough, we climbed onto the barstools, waiting for the food. Clint filled his glass with milk and started drinking it while I begged him to fill my little glass up for me, too.

A supper of warm homemade spaghetti, canned green beans, and fresh garlic bread was set on the table. My dad put a Kenny Rogers album on the record player to play as Mom dished spaghetti with meatballs and green beans onto my plate. She then gave Clint a plate of plain spaghetti noodles with butter on them. Clint's taste buds were ruined because of all the cancer treatments and medicine that he'd taken over the years, so his food preferences varied greatly from the rest of us. He still loved garlic bread, though, so he loaded his plate with that to accompany his buttered noodles. I hurried and grabbed a piece of garlic bread for myself before he ate it all.

Dad woke Cody up and sat him in his high chair. We bowed our heads, closed our eyes, and waited for Dad to speak. "Lord, thank you for this food that we are about to receive. May you continue to guide and protect us in your ways, amen. Now, let's eat."

Each of us took our first few bites, savoring the flavors and we all noticed that Cody was too tired to eat. He fell asleep in his high chair without a care in the world. We oohed and aahed over him for a bit, then Clint spoke up, telling us all about his day at school.

He carried on and on about how he beat all his friends at Pencil Pop during recess, a game that a lot of kids would play at school. The object of it was to break someone's pencil with the flick of the pencil you were holding while the other kid held his pencil lengthwise between their two hands. Somehow, Clint always won at that game, too. That's just who he was, I guess, a winner of games.

Mom was a teacher's aide, and she talked about the wonderful students in her class. Her dark brown eyes sparkled as she mentioned many of them by name. She loved her students as if they were her own and seemed to really enjoy working with their sixth-grade teacher. As that year went on, I began to think of many of her students as my friends or even siblings. Since they were so special to her, they became important to me, too. The passion that she acquired through that job as an aide would lead her to become an amazing classroom teacher later in life.

School…my mom and my brother talking about that reminded me of my own day. The conversation with the lunch card lady was still heavy on my heart, but I wasn't sure why. I continued eating my supper, trying to think of a way to contribute to the conversation without making anyone sad. My family was so happy talking about their day, and I didn't want that feeling to change. For some reason, I knew that the lunch card lady conversation might make that happy feeling go away.

And then, there it came again, the impossibility of my being able to hold my thoughts in for any length of time. I had practiced and continue to practice to this day, but there comes a point when the dam breaks, and my thoughts come trickling out of my mouth like a slow-moving river trying to navigate its way through the land. That day was no different. Moving slowly, cautiously, out my thoughts came.

"Do you guys know the lunch card lady at school? You know, the one who takes the cards before we get our trays?"

Stares.

Mom, Dad, and Clint all waited intently for me to finish what I had to say because they probably knew there was more coming, so I continued.

"She always asks me the same question every time I see her, 'How is your brother doing?'"

More stares as they all continued to wait.

"Today I told her that Clint's cancer was back. She looked at me funny and said that she already knew that but wanted to know how he was. What did she mean?"

Like mother, like daughter, keeping words locked inside was impossible. "His cancer is back. She already knows that—the whole town knows that. She should just let you eat your lunch."

Without hesitation, my dad spoke up, "Relax, Boop." He patted her leg. "That was nice of her to share her concern."

Mom took a deep breath and added, "Yes. She was just being nice. Maybe she just wanted to know how he was feeling."

"I feel fine." Clint piped in.

"But are you really fine?" I asked my brother.

"Sure. I mean, my nose bleeds a lot, and I feel sick sometimes, but today I'm fine. I'll tell her that when I see her again. I'll tell her that I'm going to be fine."

"Okay," I was satisfied with his answer.

We all went back to eating our supper as the conversation turned to my dad being silly. He grabbed a spaghetti noodle with his fingers and tried to suck it up as fast as he could without chewing it. My brother and I laughed and tried to do the same. Mom quietly finished eating her spaghetti. It wasn't something that she liked eating, but she made it because she knew it was one of my dad's favorites. Every day, we tried as a family to make each other happy, and we each had our own way of making that happen.

BEDTIME

AFTER SUPPER WAS OVER, we all helped to clean up the kitchen. Clint cleaned off the table and swept the yellow and white flowered linoleum floor while Mom woke Cody up and got him to eat. When Cody was done eating, she placed him in his playpen, then wrapped up all the leftovers from dinner in aluminum foil and put them away in our mustard-yellow colored fridge. Dad and I were busy doing the dishes. I was still too short to reach the sink, so I stood on a chair. Dad washed everything while I rinsed each dish and placed them in the rack to dry. Dad would teasingly splash a little water on my hands to try and hurry me along. I would sometimes get distracted admiring the soap bubbles on my hands and forget what I was supposed to be doing. In just a short amount of time, and with help from each other, the evening chores were completed. "Is it time for *Emergency* yet?" I asked

Mom nodded. "It sure is. It's almost 6:00."

I ran into the living room and turned on our TV, a big wooden box that sat on the floor. I turned the round knob to the correct channel, then stood back a little way to see if the picture was clear.

It was a little fuzzy, so I had Clint help me adjust the long metal rabbit ears until the picture was as clear as it could possibly be.

After the TV was set, Clint dragged our big green bean bag chair to the middle of the living room, and we both climbed on it. I loved how the little white beads inside the bag conformed perfectly to our bodies when we sat on the chair; Mom had sewn it by hand. We watched the commercials patiently waiting for my favorite show to start.

"Why do you like this show so much?" Clint asked staring right at me.

"I don't know. Just because." I wondered to myself why I liked the show so much.

He poked me in the side. "Maybe it's because the guys on the show are firefighters like Dad. Or maybe because you think the guys are cute."

"I do *not* think they're cute," I protested, knowing very well that he already knew I thought John, one of the main characters, was really cute. I'd mentioned Johnny's name so many times in the past that everyone who knew me understood that I thought I was going to marry him one day, when I was old enough.

Looking back, though, I think watching that show helped me process the kind of things that my dad encountered on some of the fire calls he went on. The hospital aspect of the show helped me to understand some of the procedures and things that my big brother, Clint, had to endure. Knowing was much easier for me than not knowing. Knowledge is power.

Finally, the red light flashing on top of the red rescue truck appeared on the screen, and the loud siren could be heard, indicating the start of the show. Clint watched it with me until the first commercial came on, then he got bored and ran off into our bedroom to play with his model train.

I sat in the big green bean bag chair all by myself for the next hour, intently watching the rest of the show. I wasn't in the room alone, though. Mom was sitting in one of our new, matching set of soft gold fabric-colored rocking chairs she and Dad purchased just a few weeks before Cody was born. The gold chairs were a bright contrast to the dark green hand-me-down leather couch that sat next to them in the living room. Mom was busy crocheting a new blanket for Clint while also watching TV. She never said it out loud, but I think she secretly thought John was cute, too.

My dad was in the family room watching Cody while listening to a record with the volume down low, strumming his guitar. Our house was large enough that the sound from the TV and the record player didn't clash with each other. Or if they did, I didn't notice.

After *Emergency* was over, I ran off to meet up with Clint in our bedroom. My big brother and I shared a bedroom so that our new little brother could have his own. The walls were made with the same wood paneling as the rest of the house. Clint's and my room was lined with Dad's baseball and football pennants that had hung in his bedroom when he was a boy. The blue and white Baltimore Colts pennant, the red and gold San Francisco 49ers pennant, and the purple and gold Minnesota Vikings pennants are the ones that stood out the most with their bold colors.

Our bedroom was where we kept all our favorite things. I had my dolls, My Little Ponies, and a little plastic Fisher Price record player that would keep me happy for hours. My brother had his Hot Wheels and his train that kept him busy when he wasn't trying to crash into my dolls with his cars or toss my little plastic records around like Frisbees. It's a wonder how any of my toys survived his multiple attacks.

Clint had a tall wooden bed that my dad had built from scratch. On his bed was a Star Wars bedspread adorned with Luke Skywalker, Han Solo, Jabba the Hutt, and Chewbacca. On the wall above his bed was a poster of Chewbacca that always scared me when the lights were off. With the way my imagination worked, in the dark, Chewbacca transformed into a black monster.

My brother would laugh at how much it scared me. "He's looking at you and is going to come and get you while you're sleeping."

That helped, not at all.

Clint was busy playing with his trains when I walked into our bedroom. My dad had built my brother's bed tall enough to place a large piece of plywood below it that Clint used as his train table. He and Dad would spend hours together building houses, placing the track in just the right spot, and watching the train go around and around. While they worked, I would sometimes hide underneath the table and play with my dolls, imagining that the train was taking us all on an adventure somewhere far away.

My bed was a white painted wooden hand-me-down that some family friends had given me when I was four years old. When I got my new bed, Mom let me pick out a sheet, pillowcase, comforter, and curtain set from the Sears catalog. She told me that I could have any comforter set that I wanted. It was the first time in my life I had ever picked out something completely on my own. I looked through the Sears catalog for hours trying to decide on the perfect set. Finally, I settled on a white bedspread featuring all the Disney characters enjoying a bright, sunny day. Mickey, Minnie, Pluto, Donald, and Goofy lit up my side of the room for several years with their cheerful grins. My bedspread continued to comfort me many different times in my life, bringing joy to my heart on some of the darkest days. Sometimes, parents have no idea how the smallest decisions in life can help their children in ways they never imagined.

After an hour or so of playing in our room, Mom came in to tell us that it was time for bed. We tried to procrastinate for a bit by going into the living room and pretending to be really interested in whatever was on TV.

"Okay, you two, it's time for bed," she reminded us.

Finally, Clint and I hurried to brush our teeth and change into our pajamas. I sat on my bed wearing my favorite pink nightgown with butterflies, while reading stories to my dolls. Clint played with his train in his *Star Wars* pajamas. We were supposed to be in bed but fought off bedtime while we waited for our parents to come and tuck us in for the night.

Dad came in first to tell us that we'd be getting up extra early the next day. We would be making the long drive from our house, just outside of Livingston, all the way to the city of Oakland, California. We were taking Clint in for treatments at the Children's Hospital there.

"How early do we have to get up?" I asked, eagerly awaiting an answer.

"5:00 a.m. before the sun comes up."

"Yay! I'll get to look out the window at the stars while we're driving."

"Yep, and if it's not too foggy, we can watch the sunrise through the mirrors and out the back window."

"My favorite part."

"Do we get Pop-Tarts?" asked Clint.

Dad laughed. "Sure, why not?"

With that, my brother climbed up the wooden ladder to his bed, and I crawled under the covers in mine. Dad kissed us both goodnight and then headed back to the living room. My brother chattered away about which flavor Pop-Tart he would eat in the morning while we waited for Mom to come in. He was having trouble deciding between brown sugar, cherry, or strawberry.

Mom overheard our conversation and added to it as she walked into our bedroom. "You guys don't even like Pop-Tarts."

"Yes we do." said Clint. "The icing on top is the best."

"The icing? That's all you eat, then you throw the rest away."

I said, "I like the middle part where the fruit is. It's soft and sweet."

"But neither of you eats the crust. We end up throwing most of the Pop-Tarts away because you only eat parts of them."

Clint and I looked at each other, and then I commented that at least we would eat some of it. "Maybe we can share the parts that we don't eat with you and Dad."

With that, Mom smiled and said we could talk more about it in the morning, but for now, it was time for us to go to sleep. She tucked us both in under our covers and kissed us goodnight. As she walked out of the room, she turned off the light and reminded us to try to get some rest because the next day would be busy with doctor appointments.

I hated it when the lights went out. I hated the dark. As soon as she left the room, I jumped out of my bed and climbed up the ladder to my brother's. Sleeping was something that never came easily for me, so my brother would let me lie next to him while he quietly told me stories until I was tired enough to crawl back into my own bed. Besides, when I lay in my brother's bed, I couldn't see the scary black monster Chewbacca poster looking at me.

Clint told me stories about school, his friends, and how he would drive a big rig truck one day. I listened intently as pictures formed in my mind with each story. I loved listening to him talk because it meant that he wasn't feeling sick. When he was feeling really awful, he didn't talk at all. As we lay there, we heard the TV go off, we heard Mom and Dad put Cody in his crib in the nursery, and the lights in the rest of the house switched off.

It had been a busy day, so it didn't take long before I was finally tired enough to crawl back into my own bed. Clint was sound asleep before I even got settled under my Mickey Mouse and friends comforter. I listened to the absolute silence that surrounded me. Nobody was talking, no dogs were barking, and no cars were passing by on the road in front of our house. All that could be heard was the absolute stillness that being out in the middle of nowhere brings.

It was so quiet that I could hear my own heart beating. I wondered how I could make it a little softer. The sound of it was like a booming drum in the stillness of the night. I tried holding my breath as I looked out the window. That was harder than I thought, and it didn't stop the loud beating of my heart. I quickly filled my lungs with air as I watched the fog swirl around the dimly lit dusk-to-dawn light that stood tall near the Quonset hut. The fog would settle deep in the Central Valley that night, and I wondered if I'd be able to see any stars on our drive in the morning. I really didn't like the fog because it blocked out all the light. Not being able to see any source of light scared me.

I focused on the little piece of light that I could still see illuminating from the dusk-to-dawn light. It brought a smile to my face as I slowly closed my eyes, breathed with the rhythm of my beating heart, and drifted off to sleep.

THE DRIVE

Each day brings new hope, new joy, new love.
~KIMBERLEY'S THOUGHT~

IT WAS TIME for us to watch the sunrise as we made the long journey to the hospital in the big city. I changed out of my nightgown into my good clothes as quickly as I could. That day I wore dark brown corduroy pants and a long-sleeved train shirt, both of which used to be my brother's. I hated those pants because they made noise when I walked. It vibrated my ears and made me feel as if the whole world could hear me walking.

But they were warm, and Mom really liked them on me. The train shirt was awful as well. It was light brown and covered in train cars of all different colors that were in vertical rows, front and back. I thought it made me look like a boy. The only reason I ever agreed to wear it was for Clint. He loved it and hated that it didn't fit him anymore.

When I wore it, he'd spend the whole day telling everyone, "Do you like my sister's shirt? That used to be mine."

I'd give my biggest smile because I knew it made him happy. Deep down, though, I couldn't wait until it didn't fit me anymore.

Clint stayed comfortable in his pajamas. There was no reason for him to change into regular clothes because he'd probably be spending the day in a hospital bed. And chances were that he'd have to change into a gown as soon as we got there anyway. Besides, he'd be more comfortable in his pajamas on the long car ride. It was best for him to be comfortable because then he'd be able to sleep more easily if he needed to. He was often tired and needed his rest.

It didn't take us long to get ready to go, as we'd all made this journey several times before. Clint and I had our blankets wrapped around us, and Clint had his orange kidney-shaped vomit bucket in case he got sick on the drive. Cody was sound asleep in his car seat that was wedged between Clint and me and looked as cozy as could be. Once we were all settled in our seats, Mom handed Clint and me a Pop-Tart. The neighbors could probably see our white teeth through the thick fog because of how big our smiles were. We'd hit the jackpot!

Mom made us promise to try and eat the whole thing because they were expensive, and we didn't have the money for her and my dad to buy food that we weren't going to eat. Clint and I promised to do our best as we peeled back the silver metal wrapper to unveil our special breakfast treat. The white frosting with little red sprinkles told us that they were cherry Pop-Tarts, my favorite.

We could all hear soft country music playing on the radio as my dad drove our little blue Toyota Corolla onto the main country road. Clint and I slowly chewed each bite of our Pop-Tarts, savoring the flavor as if it were the first time we'd ever eaten one in our lives. We even managed to eat all the crust parts that day as well. Later in life, I learned that if the Pop-Tarts were cooked in the toaster, then the crust was crunchy and sweet instead of soft and tasteless. I really wish I'd have known that when I was five.

As we traveled along, I stared out the window with my face pointed toward the sky. I tried hard to spot a star through the dense fog. I just knew there had to be one that would peek its way through, and I was determined to find it. After an hour or so of driving, we were in heavy traffic, but the fog had disappeared. Now was my chance. The perfect time to see a star was before the sun started to rise. My brothers were both asleep, Mom had her eyes closed, but I knew she wasn't actually sleeping. Dad was humming along to a song that was playing on the radio, and I sat contently with my big doll in my lap.

My big doll had been a special surprise from my mom. It had been just an ordinary spring day when I was only four, several months before my little brother was born. That morning, my mom took me to the neighbor's house down the street as she'd done many times before. The neighbors were friends of our family, but the mom in the family was also my babysitter for a short time. Most days when I went there, I would play with the youngest son in the family, who was close to my age. His mom watched both of us while his two older brothers and my big brother were all at school.

On that special day, I'd only been at the neighbor's house for a few hours before there was a knock at the door. The neighbor boy and I were watching *Sesame Street* when my mom picked me up. Instead of driving me home, she drove me to the department store about thirty minutes away from our house. She took me there to pick out a doll. Before that time, my special doll was my little yellow Baby Beans. I took it with me everywhere. That doll was to me what some would consider to be their special baby blanket; my comfort toy. She was my best friend, I told her all my secrets, and she helped me fall asleep at night. She was the only doll that I'd ever known until that day in the department store.

As we walked into the store, Mom led me straight to the area where all the toys were. It was a rarity for us to go to a department store, so I wandered the aisle in awe of all that surrounded me. I was looking at the dolls when Mom told me to pick out any one I wanted.

My eyes widened. "For real?"

"For real. It's time that you had a new doll to be friends with, Baby Beans." She said with a little laughter in her voice. I'm sure she knew I'd be surprised to hear those words, and I could tell she was overjoyed with happiness, seeing the excitement on my face.

She tried to show me the difference between some of the dolls, but it only took me a second to spot the one that I wanted. It was a very realistic-looking doll with a cloth body, thick plastic arms and legs, and a hard plastic head with eyes that opened and closed when I moved its head back and forth. She was dressed in a white baby dress with pink frills. She was perfect. She was roughly the size of a newborn baby and was almost too large for me to carry, but I didn't care. I'd drag her around with me if I had to.

My mom carefully put the box containing my big doll in the shopping cart as we headed toward the checkout stand.

"Are we going to get anything else?"

"Nope. We just came for this."

"Really? Why?"

"Because you're soon going to have a new baby brother or sister, and I wanted you to pick out something special just for you. Something new for you to take care of that's all yours."

"You're going to have a baby?"

"I am. And it will be here soon. You can use your new doll to practice having a new baby in the house."

I tried to absorb what my mom was telling me as she paid for my new doll. A new baby brother or sister? Such excitement that brought to my heart, but also a little fear of what the change in our family might be like. As soon as we got to the car, Mom took my new doll out of the package, and I held her tightly in my arms the whole ride home. My new doll was all mine.

I named her Breanna for a short time, then changed it again and again, but usually I just always referred to her as my big doll.

After that day, I took her with me everywhere that I could. The hospital included. Such a special memory Mom had created for me in sharing the news of how I would soon be a big sister.

I held my doll in my lap, replaying that memory in my mind as we drove to the hospital that morning. I continued to scan the sky for any hint of starlight. I just knew there had to be a star out there somewhere. Then finally, I saw it.

I whispered, "A star! Daddy, do you see the star?"

"I do, Sunshine, I do. Try and count how many other ones you can see."

I loved it when my daddy called me Sunshine because I loved sunshine; the opposite of darkness, it made me happy. I beamed like a beacon of light as we journeyed along, inching closer to the city while I counted the stars. I did see a lot more of them, and they were beautiful. I also saw a sliver of the moon, which shone with just a touch of brightness. Before long, I noticed how the world was beginning to wake up as the darkness turned to light and the stars slowly faded away.

"Can you see it, Kimmers, can you see the sun rising behind us?"

Even though I had my seatbelt on, I was able to turn my body just enough to peek out the back window.

"I see it, Daddy, I see it."

I saw that he watched it out the rearview mirror as I watched it out the back window. Mom opened her eyes, and I saw her peer at the beautiful rising sun in the passenger side mirror. Clint woke up just in time to see the sun fully rise over the Sierra Nevada mountains that were now very far off in the distance. Cody slept peacefully through the whole ordeal, which was a good thing because he was very restless whenever he was awake and strapped into his car seat. As we witnessed the moment when night turned into day, for an instant, all was right in the world.

Clint broke the calm silence. "I need a tissue."

His nose was bleeding, which happened often. Every time I saw his nose bleeding, it reminded me of the story Mom told me about how they first discovered Clint had leukemia. It was on New Year's Day, and he was only four years old at the time. My parents were planning on spending that day at my grandparents' house, celebrating the new year and watching college football. On their drive from the foothills to the valley, Clint's nose started bleeding profusely. They couldn't get it to stop and had a gut feeling that something was terribly wrong. They felt it best to stop at the closest hospital to get help.

Call it mother's intuition or the power of knowledge, but Mom felt that there was something much more wrong with Clint than just a bloody nose. As soon as they got to the hospital, she suggested to the doctors that Clint be tested for cancer. Shortly after stopping at the hospital, Clint was rushed by ambulance to a larger hospital in the valley. Mom again encouraged the doctors to test for cancer. She had read an article in *Reader's Digest* when she was young about a girl who had leukemia. She was reminded of that article when she saw the bruises on Clint's legs and a bloody nose that wouldn't stop. Doctors followed her lead and informed my parents that Clint did indeed have leukemia, a type of blood cancer.

At that time, the five-year survival rate for Acute Lymphoblastic Leukemia (ALL) was less than 10 percent. My parents were devastated by the news but were determined to do everything in their power to help him survive. As time went on, Clint had defied the odds and surprised some of the most brilliant doctors with treatments they used, such as chemotherapy, radiation, and experimental medicines. There were many times when my parents had been told to say their final goodbyes to my brother because he wasn't expected to make it through the night. Clint was a brave little boy, though, and was able to fight off fevers, staph infections, chicken pox, countless bone marrow depressions, two blood clots on his brain, as well as all the normal childhood cuts and bruises, and illnesses, all while battling leukemia.

After years of fighting the disease, doctors were successful at finally putting Clint's cancer into remission, only to have it come back again. This time, it had spread to other parts of his body. So, our family was on the way to the hospital, ready to embrace whatever doctors had planned to help Clint continue his battle against cancer. A battle that we were all in together.

THE HOSPITAL

WALKING THROUGH the front doors of the hospital felt like walking into a friend's house that I'd been in a thousand times before. I walked down the long white hallway surrounded by the familiar smell of rubbing alcohol and cleaning solutions. There were always lots of people. Some of the faces I'd seen before, and others I was seeing for the very first time. Several were walking steadily as if they knew exactly where they were going, but in no huge hurry to get there. Others were moving about frantically as if they'd completely forgotten where they were. It was a sight that I'd seen so many times before.

I can't remember the first time we went to what we called Oakland Children's Hospital, its actual name was Children's Hospital Oakland. I had been going there with my family my entire life. We knew almost all the nurses and doctors by their first names. We also knew the cooks in the cafeteria, the janitorial staff, the long-term patients, other families that frequently visited the hospital, and where all the waiting and restrooms were. There were always lots of things to do at that giant kids' hospital.

I ran ahead to the wall where the kids' pictures were. They had drawn them during their stay in the hospital. On the wall to the right, just out of my five-year-old arm's length, was a picture that my brother had drawn with crayons. It was in a silver metal frame. I can't remember all the details, but I know for certain there was a bright yellow sun in the right-hand corner. He drew it during one of his many stays. CLINT was in the bottom right corner in big black letters. I admired that picture, so proud that it made it onto the wall. I wondered if one of my pictures would ever be placed beside my big brother's.

My family finally caught up with me and scooted me along to the doctor's office. We couldn't all fit in the tiny room where my brother was being examined, so Mom went to the waiting room with Cody. Clint, Dad, and I went into the exam room to wait for the doctor. When I was given the option, I always chose to go into the exam room with Clint because it was more fun than just sitting in the waiting room. Somehow, someway, my dad always made the exam room feel like an amusement park.

As soon as we got in there, Clint and I went straight to the long metal pedals underneath the sink and put our feet on them. They controlled the hot and cold water that came out of the faucet. My brother, Dad, and I took turns pressing on the pedals and counted how long it took before the water would start pouring into the sink. It fascinated us that there was a bit of delay.

Then, we spent the next few minutes pretending like we were surgeons in desperate need of having to thoroughly wash our hands. After that, Dad grabbed a set of white gloves from the box by the sink and put them on. The surgical masks were also in a box by the sink. Dad put one on and pretended he was a doctor, all prepped to begin surgery. Next, he took off the gloves and blew into each of them like they were balloons. He let go of them, and they flew around the room for a second while Clint and I tried to catch them.

Now that we were all hyped up, it was Dad's job to calm us down. After all, we were in a doctor's office.

He sat down. "All right, we'd better chill out."

He threw the gloves into the garbage can, and Clint hopped up onto the bed. I sat in a chair next to the sink, and Dad quietly opened the little metal door under the bed.

"Oh no! We'd better keep that door closed because monkeys are in there," he whispered.

"Monkeys?" Clint and I squealed.

"Yeah, lots of them."

Clint climbed off the bed and cautiously opened the door. "There are monkeys in there, but I can't see how many because it's too dark."

I jumped off my chair. "I wanna see!"

Dad pretended to look all over the room. "We need to find a flashlight. That will help us see better so we can count how many there are." He held up a blood pressure cuff that he pulled off the wall. "How about this?"

"No. That won't work," said Clint.

I shook my head.

Dad pulled the otoscope off the wall, the thing the doctor used to check our ears. He pushed the button to turn its light on. "How about this?"

"Yes! That will work," I said.

"Oh no, it won't reach." Dad shared the news with disappointment. It was attached to the wall and wouldn't quite reach all the way to where the monkeys were hiding.

When the doctor entered the room, we were all examining the wall to see if there was a way to take the otoscope off. She laughed because she'd seen these antics played out by us several times before. It seemed that Dad's purpose in life was to do anything he could to make us kids laugh before the doctor came in. He sometimes got in trouble with the doctor, but being reprimanded didn't seem to bother him as long as we were happy.

My brother was being admitted to the hospital, so after the exam was over, we all made our way to Clint's room on the fifth floor. As we made our journey down hallways and up elevators, we passed other kids and their families. Some were walking with their IVs in tow, others were scooting along in the big plastic red toy cars that I'd only ever seen at the hospital, and others were walking hand in hand with their parents or nurses.

We spent the next hour meeting with doctors while Clint was being poked, prodded, and having IVs started. We were led to his new room by one of our favorite nurses. When we entered, I ran to the window seat to claim my spot with a view of the outside world. Not every room that Clint had been in had window seats, but these were my favorite. I could look out and watch everything the sky had to offer; clouds, the sun, moon, stars, and even an occasional airplane flying by.

Mom sat in the chair that was closest to the bed, while Clint got settled in. He was busy with the big white rectangular TV remote that was attached to his bed with a long white cord. He flipped through the channels, trying to find something to watch on the big brown box that was mounted high on the wall at the foot of his bed. The remote also controlled what his bed would do. He could push the buttons to move the head or the foot up and down.

Dad walked out into the hallway carrying Cody. He said he wanted to see other patients who were in rooms close by. He wanted to say, hi and to let them know we were there.

I sat in the window seat looking out at the sea of buildings that surrounded us. It was a bright sunny day in the Bay Area, so there weren't any clouds to look at or interesting weather to observe. I quickly became bored with trying to see what the sky had to offer, so instead, I spent the next few hours soaking in the sunshine while I colored, read books, played with my big doll, and tried to watch TV with Clint. I was always glad that Mom and Dad brought things for me to do while we were at the hospital.

After a while, Clint fell asleep, and the rest of us were hungry, so we went down to the cafeteria to get some lunch. We didn't want to wake Clint up, so we quietly snuck out of the room without him seeing us. We always felt bad when we'd have to leave him behind, but he probably wouldn't have eaten anything except chocolate pudding anyway. And we could easily bring him that.

We took the elevator down to what felt like the basement, then walked through a long hallway to get to the place where we'd be eating. The hospital cafeteria was a dark place that felt like a long-forgotten room in the deepest, darkest part of the building. It was the furthest thing away from Clint's bright, sunny room.

Red and blue trays were stacked at the entrance of the cafeteria. The smell of hamburgers and hot dogs cooking on the grill filled the room. We picked out a few things to eat from the long silver metal cafeteria food counter, paid, then sat at a table in the middle of the room. We were surrounded by doctors, nurses, patients, and other hospital workers who were all hurriedly eating as if counting down the seconds before they needed to be somewhere else. The four of us ate our food in silence while Mom and Dad took turns making sure that Cody was chewing his food completely before swallowing.

"Remember to chew, chew, chew," Mom reminded him.

The cafeteria was bustling with noise and people, but I couldn't clearly understand a single word. When we were finished eating, we quickly headed back to Clint's room to see how he was doing.

He was awake, but we couldn't see much of him at all. He was holding up his big brown monkey puppet, Coco, in front of his face. Coco's long arms and legs were dangling down in front of Clint's body.

"Hi-roe," Coco said in his scratchy monkey voice.

"Hi, Coco," I said, and Cody and I ran over to give Coco a big hug.

I really thought Coco could talk until one day when I saw Clint's mouth moving and realized that it was Clint who had been talking for him. Clint, Coco, Cody, and I had spent a lot of time together in Clint's different hospital rooms over the years. Coco was a special gift that the doctors had given to Clint to help make his days a little brighter, and he loved introducing Coco to everyone. He especially loved to show him off to the Oakland A's baseball players when they came to visit the patients.

Soon, a nurse and a doctor came into the room. We all said our hellos to each other before Mom guided Cody and I out of the room. We rode the elevator to the first floor and walked down the long hall where Clint's picture was. Then we stopped at the big play area where we were greeted by Freida, one of my favorite hospital workers. She enveloped me in her arms and led me to a chair at a table.

"Have fun!" Mom said. "I'm going to drop Cody off in the nursery then head back to Clint's room."

Freida kept me busy drawing pictures with me, playing games, and reading books. She then led me to a tall metal cabinet where the toys were kept. She let me choose any toy that I wanted to play with. I chose a little cloth doll that was wearing pink pants and a frilly pink shirt. Freida found a little plastic bottle with a pink plastic top that looked as if it had milk inside. Then, she picked up a similar one that looked like it had orange juice in it. She led me back to the table and showed me how to pull the string on the doll's back. When I did, the baby doll's body moved, duplicating the motion a real baby would make while eating from a bottle. Frieda then had me put the milk bottle in the doll's mouth. I was shocked to see that when I did that, the doll started to drink milk from the bottle! The doll wasn't really drinking the milk, but it sure was fun to pretend she was. Freida and I played with the doll for what felt like hours before she helped me put it back in the metal cabinet.

A short time later, Dad arrived with Cody in his arms to pick me up. We walked back to Clint's hospital room. After a long day, it was time for Mom, Dad, Cody, and me to leave so that he could get plenty of rest. We said goodbye to him and made our way back to the parking lot, where we gathered back into our blue Toyota Corolla. Dad drove us out of the parking lot and onto the streets of Oakland. It didn't take long before he was quickly weaving in and out of traffic as if he were a professional NASCAR driver.

"We're going so fast!"

Mom said to me, "He sometimes forgets that he's not driving the fire truck."

Since Dad was a volunteer firefighter in our tiny town, he spent many hours driving the fire truck through traffic. He had also been born and raised in San Francisco, so he knew his way around the city streets and the cities in the surrounding area like the back of his hand.

My dad always loved to reminisce and show us the sights of his youth when we were in the area, and there was still enough daylight left in the day for him to do just that. So, he drove us out of Oakland and into San Francisco. He pointed out the first home of the San Francisco 49ers and the Oakland Raiders, the original Kezar Stadium. He talked with excitement as he told us stories about how he would attend games there before the 49ers started playing at Candlestick Park.

We drove past the Golden Gate Bridge and into Golden Gate Park. He showed Cody and me the exact spot where he used to play football with his friends. As he talked, I looked for the lake where my grandpa taught him how to fish. Next, the peaceful drive past the house in the Sunset District that he lived in until he was eighteen but was now filled with strangers.

Dad took a lot of pride in showing us kids where all his favorite spots were. Mom had seen them many times before.

I suddenly remembered how thrilling it was to ride down the really steep street in San Francisco that had lots of twists and turns to it. "Can we go down the fun street?"

"What street do you think is really fun?" Dad asked.

"You know, the red brick one."

"Oh, she's talking about Lombard Street," said Mom. "Are you thinking of the crookedest street in the world?"

"Yeah, that one. Can we go down it?"

"I don't think we'll have time today. We'll have to save that for next time." Dad drove into another part of the city that used to be *his*.

We went down a few more streets, and Dad chatted away telling us stories about Solari's Grill, the restaurant that his dad once owned on Geary Street. He told us about the people who used to dine there and talked with pride about how his dad had only spoken French when he immigrated from Switzerland but quickly learned to speak English and did his best to assimilate into the American way of life.

"I want to learn French," I blurted.

Dad laughed. "Un, deux, trois. That's about all the French I know."

"What's that mean?" I asked curiously

He laughed again. "One, two, three."

I spent the next several minutes trying to count to three in

French. We drove into Daly City to make a stop at my Grandma Ghiggia's small apartment to give her a quick hello hug.

"Hi, Genie!" she said to my dad as we walked into her apartment. She loved calling Dad Genie, even though he hated that nickname and quickly reminded her that his name was Gene.

Grandma Ghiggia carefully pulled her gold-wired rimmed glasses away from her steel gray hazel eyes, careful not to get them caught in her curly gray hair. She kept them attached to a chain that hung like a necklace around her neck. She sat on her bed and held Cody for a few minutes admiring his big, beautiful brown eyes. Then she handed him over to Dad, gave us all hugs, and told us to stop by again soon as we made our way out the door.

The next stop was at my Uncle Johnny's house in South San Francisco. We stopped by there for a short visit to say hello to my dad's brother, my aunt, and cousins before we left the streets of South San Francisco and drove back across the Bay Bridge to Concord where we'd be spending the night with my dad's childhood friends, Rod and Donna.

Dad parked the car in the driveway. We'd been there many times before, and I jumped out of the car with anticipation of seeing my favorite wall in the entryway of the house. Besides the people that lived inside, the wall of mirrors was my favorite part of this stop. It made the entryway and step-down living room feel like a stage filled with so much joy and light where the whole world was watching.

We were greeted with open arms by our family friends. Dad had known Rod and Donna most of his life. They were married now, with three children of their own, and were happy to share their home with us.

We stood in the entryway and talked for a few minutes before being led into their kitchen for dinner. We spent the rest of the evening eating, watching TV, playing games, and visiting. Their home was a happy place filled with so much warmth. And though we all missed Clint, being at their home was a nice reprieve from the hustle and bustle of the hospital.

As the evening drew to a close, the hide-a-bed in the step-down living room was pulled out for us to sleep on. It was exciting to have a sleepover at our friends' house. I was almost too excited to fall asleep, but it had been a busy day, so I was really tired. I thought about how Clint must be having fun watching his own TV with Coco in his hospital bed, as I snuggled up between my mom and dad on the hide-a-bed and fell fast asleep.

Clint with his puppet Coco.

STAYING WITH OTHERS

Those who walk with us in the darkness
are the keepers of light.

IT HAD BEEN SEVERAL DAYS since I had snuggled between my parents in the hide-a-bed and life had been anything but normal. The only normalcy in my life was that I still went to school each day during the week to see my friends. The lunch card lady still asked me daily how my brother was, and since I really didn't know, I simply answered, "I don't know."

She looked at me sympathetically while I moved through the lunch line. It was a little harder to utter the words, "I don't know," instead of my usual, "fine," because not actually knowing how my brother was doing was an uncomfortable thought.

My parents tried hard to ensure that at least one of them was able to be home for a few days at a time, so they took turns staying at the hospital with Clint. There were some nights, though, that I didn't see either of them because they both needed to stay in Oakland. That required me to stay someplace other than at home on those nights. At least I always had my big doll and my

Baby Beans with me to keep me company.

I stood at the edge of the koi pond in the backyard our family friends, Bill and Donna. I watched the huge white, orange, and black speckled fish meander their way up and down the full length of the large cement pond. A wooden pergola and limbs from trees gave the fish just the right amount of shade. Water bubbled from the pumps, helping to aerate the water to keep the fish healthy and happy, and the smell of wet moss filled the air.

Bill, with his dark brown hair, wire-rimmed glasses, and standing much taller than my dad, towered over me as he handed me a handful of fish food. I dropped the brown pellets into the pond one by one as the fish scrambled to the surface to be the lucky one to gobble it up before the others could get to it. Bill showed me how I could just throw a handful of food to the fish, but I preferred to do it my way. It made the food last longer, and I took joy in watching them try to figure out where I would throw the next food pellet. Bill laughed at my decision and told me to have fun.

I spent the next thirty minutes or so methodically deciding where to throw the next pellet and just watching the fish swim about in the pond. After the last one I brushed my hands together to get the crumbs of fish food off. Then I went into the house, where I passed by Bill, who was now relaxing in his chair, reading a book.

"Hi, kiddo. Are the fish all done eating?" he asked.

I smiled as I walked past him. "Yep."

I found Donna sitting at the kitchen table, grading papers. "There you are. Come here, you." She pulled me in for a big hug. Her largely curled strawberry blond hair fell in my face as she embraced me in her arms. "Do you want to help me grade papers?"

"Can I?"

"Sure, why not?" She grabbed a green marker from her teacher bag.

"Here it is. Now, all you have to do is put a big smiley face or a star at the top of each paper, just like this." She demonstrated on a few papers before handing the marker to me and my own stack of her students' papers. I struggled with making a star, so she showed me over and over how to do it until I seemed to have mastered it.

"You've got it. You're going to make a great teacher one day."

I beamed, thinking about how amazing that would be.

I had fun pretending like I was a teacher correcting the papers of big third graders. I drew my best smiley face or star on the top of each paper as if creating a tiny masterpiece for each student.

Donna worked hard, carefully checking over her students' work in her own stack of papers while occasionally checking on me to see if I was marking each paper correctly. I felt like such a grown-up as I sat quietly beside her. When I got to third grade, she was my teacher, and I was encouraged to call her Mrs. Grunloh instead of Donna. I abided by that rule while I was at school and respected her as my teacher, but everywhere outside of school, she was always like another mom to me.

Bill and Donna were never able to have any children of their own, but they always made me feel as if I were one of theirs. I loved them with my whole heart and was overjoyed anytime I was able to be around them. They were sometimes my babysitters when my parents were at the hospital with Clint, and during those times, they did everything they could to help me keep my mind off the reality of what was happening with my big brother.

Bill walked into the kitchen and got something to drink. "Are you ready to go and see your grandparents?"

"Yep!" I squealed and gave Donna a hug.

Bill helped me climb into his green Volkswagen van, and he settled in the driver's seat. We made the short drive from their house on the outskirts of town to our ranch in the country. I loved riding in his van because I sat up high enough to see everything around me. Donna had a Volkswagen van, too, but hers was a rusty dark gold color. When I got older, I often rode with her to and from school.

Though I loved Bill and Donna dearly, they weren't the only adults that I spent time with. My parents struggled to balance work, school, taking care of us kids, paying bills, and simply surviving with the roller coaster of emotions that come with having a child battling cancer. When I was in school, my parents' friends would take turns having me over at their houses so that they wouldn't have to worry about me missing school. Even at times when Clint was out of the hospital, their friends would watch all of us kids so that my parents could have a weekend just to focus on each other. I didn't realize it then, but we were surrounded by family and friends who helped to shape who our family was. It often takes a village to survive.

I waved goodbye to Bill and slammed the screen door as I ran inside my grandparents' house.

"Hi, Kimmy. You're just in time for dinner." Grandma smiled as she carried three metal TV trays into their living room.

I followed her to where Papa was putting another log on the fire. He turned the TV on and flipped through the channels until he found *Wheel of Fortune*. I had arrived just in time. It was part of their nightly routine to eat dinner right at 6:00 p.m. while watching the game program. I was overjoyed on nights that I was able to be part of that.

Grandma and Papa set up the three TV trays so that we each had our own to put our dinner on. The trays had beautiful outdoor mountain scenes on them. My grandma brought in our supper of chicken, green beans, and mashed potatoes. I followed her and Papa into the kitchen to get my little glass of milk.

Grandma smiled. "I made the chicken in my new microwave." She laughed. "Hopefully it's good. I'm still trying to figure out how to work that thing."

While we ate, I tried my best to figure out each word puzzle that came up on the screen, but I wasn't very successful. I still didn't really know how to spell yet, so my grandparents figured out all of the words before I did. I didn't mind, though, because my favorite part of the show was when the person who won each round picked out what they wanted to buy from the little showroom.

After we finished eating, we carried our dishes into the kitchen, put our TV trays away, cleaned up, then went into the living room to relax. Papa sat in his chair and watched TV while Grandma showed me how to make a latch hook rug. I watched her intently as she steadily put another piece of yarn into the little square and pulled it through. I was amazed that something so simple could turn into a beautiful, soft picture to hang on the wall.

After a while, Grandma and I went to her bedroom to play her electric organ. I sat next to her, and she taught me to play, "When the Saints Go Marching In."

She moved her fingers gently over the keys with each note, and then I copied her with my own hands. She corrected me when I hit the wrong note and showed me how to read the sheet music. I was too short to put my feet on the black foot pedal at the bottom of the organ, so she did that part for me. I loved how the organ sounded when I played each note and imagined that I was playing the song for all my family and friends to hear. I practiced that song hundreds of times after that day but could never seem to play it quite as wonderfully as my grandma did.

It was time to get ready for bed, and I stood on the soft pink rug brushing my teeth. The rug was a nice reprieve from the cold linoleum floor. The smell of Comet powder cleaner and hand soap surrounded me.

Grandma called from the kitchen. "Hurry up, Kimmy, it's time for bed."

I finished brushing my teeth, then quickly walked the short distance from the bathroom to the kitchen to get a drink of water before I made my way into the office. Grandma's office was a cozy little room right off the living room. To the left of the door was her large desk complete with a little green desk lamp. To the right, a brown, white, and orange striped couch that folded down into a bed. A window that overlooked my grandparents' yard was directly across from the door. It held many stories. One about my mom escaping from my grandpa after she'd gotten in trouble for something. Behind me were two small closets, one on each side of the door. The closets were filled to the brim with stuff. I can't say for sure what was in the closet on the right, but the closet on the left was filled with many of my favorite things.

The inside of the closet door was covered in pencil marks. Each line indicated the height that my mom, aunts, cousins, brother, and I had been at certain stages in our lives. Above each mark was the name of the person that the line represented. I opened the door and admired how tall everyone had gotten over the years. Mine were similar to my aunts, who were considered to be the shortest people in the family. Theirs showed as adults that they were each four feet, eleven inches.

"Do you want me to measure you again?" Grandma asked.

I stood as tall as I could against the door so my grandma could measure me, for the thousandth time, to prove to me that I had indeed grown a little since the last time she'd measured me. She marked the new spot with a pencil, and I grinned as she wrote Kimmy, above the new line.

She grabbed my favorite soft pink blanket out of the same closet, along with sheets and a pillow, which were above the games. I helped her convert that little couch into a bed and placed my Baby Beans and big doll on top before I snuggled with them for bed. Grandma sat next to me for a short while, telling me nursery rhymes. "Humpty Dumpty" was my favorite because it always made me laugh. She kissed my forehead and after telling me good-night, turned off the light and started to walk out of the room.

"Wait! It's dark in here."

"Oh, that's right, you don't like to sleep in the dark." She turned on the little desk lamp and started to walk out again.

Just then, Papa walked into the room and took something off the desk. "Let's use this instead." He held up a little plastic orange owl, with a plug on the back.

Grandma shrugged. "I forgot I bought that."

"This little night light won't use up quite as much energy as that desk light will." Papa plugged the night light into the wall socket right under the window. He turned off the desk lamp and ruffled my hair. "Night," he said and walked out of the office. The owl night light gave off a special orange glow.

My grandma added as she walk out of the room, "Sleep tight, don't let the bed bugs bite."

"There are bugs in here?" I jokingly asked, knowing that she didn't really mean to imply that there were bugs in my bed. We both chuckled as she closed the door behind her. I lay there and thought about what my parents and brothers were doing at that moment, knowing that they were probably at the well-lit hospital watching TV in Clint's hospital room. Sometimes my cousin Kerry would stay the night with me at my grandparents' house, but tonight wasn't one of those nights. I wished that she were lying there next to me. I repeated nursery rhymes to myself, staring at the owl night light. I slowly drifted off to sleep.

The smell of brewing coffee filled the air, telling me it was time to get up. I climbed out of bed and slowly opened the office door.

I stuck my head out just enough to peek into the kitchen to see if anyone was in there. I saw my grandpa walking toward the kitchen sink, so I knew I wouldn't be alone. I was freezing, so I quickly walked across the cold carpet and beelined it right to where the kitchen wall heater was.

"Do you want a cup of coffee?" Papa joked.

I giggled. "I can't drink coffee. My dad says that it will put hair on my chest, and I don't *want* hair on my chest."

"That's true." He chuckled. "And it will stunt your growth. You certainly don't want that to happen. You'll just be that short forever. How about hot chocolate?"

"Yeah!" I perked up. "Swiss Miss is my favorite."

The whole house smelled like bacon and coffee. While I got ready for school, Papa made me a breakfast of bacon, toast, and hot chocolate. He helped me climb up on one of the black stools at the bar. I slowly savored each bite of my food and enjoyed every sip of my hot chocolate. He leaned up against the bar, chatting away and watching me eat while he drank his coffee.

"Grandma's still busy putting her face on," he told me.

I laughed at the silly comment.

"You'd better hurry up, slowpoke, or you're going to miss the bus."

School! That's right, I needed to hurry up and walk to the bus stop.

I finished the last of my breakfast and then climbed down from the barstool. I put on my tennis shoes and jacket, then ran into my grandparents' bedroom to hug my grandma goodbye. The whole room smelled like Grandma's face powder and her perfume. She was sitting in front of the mirror, where she was putting on the last of her makeup.

She hugged me goodbye. "Have a good day!" she called as I ran out of their room.

"Watch for cars," Papa said as I said goodbye and hugged his leg.

I closed their back door tightly behind me and made the long journey to the bus stop all by myself. I kicked the dirt a little, wishing that my big brother was with me. I hated making that walk alone. At least it wasn't foggy, so that was something to be thankful for. I strolled past the almond trees, wondering when they'd wake up from their winter slumber, then reached down and picked up a stick to play with. I carried it with me to the stop sign and used it to draw pictures in the dirt until the school bus arrived.

Mr. Beasley opened the bus door and smiled. "Good Morning, kid."

"Hi, Mr. Beasley."

I walked to my favorite seat, where the heater was. A new day had begun.

SATURDAY

I LOOKED OUT my bedroom window and saw that it was foggy and still dark outside. But regardless I was wide awake. I lay there for a few minutes thinking about whether I should get up or not, then I suddenly remembered that Clint was home. He'd gotten home from the hospital just yesterday. I wasn't in our bedroom alone. I sneakily walked over to his tall bed and looked up to where he was sleeping.

I whispered, "Clint?"

"Yeah?"

"Is it time to get up yet?"

"I think so. Let's go see if cartoons are on."

He crawled over to the wooden ladder and climb down from his bed. Then we quietly snuck into the living room. Clint turned the TV on and found Saturday morning cartoons.

"They're on." I ran back into our bedroom to get my pillow and blanket, and Clint did the same. We spent the next hour content as could be lying on the living room floor watching *Bugs Bunny*, The *Smurfs*, *Scooby-Doo*, and whatever cartoon came on next.

Soon, the house started to stir, and everyone else in the family was awake.

Clint and I were thrilled that we no longer had to be quiet, so we moseyed our way into the kitchen to get cereal for breakfast. By that time, we were starving. I took the box of Lucky Charms out of the cupboard, and Clint grabbed the Coco Puffs. We set both on the breakfast bar. Clint took the gallon of milk out of our big yellow refrigerator, and I got two glass bowls out of the cupboard and carried them over to the cereal. I got us each a spoon and set those next to our bowls. I poured Lucky Charms into my bowl until it was almost overflowing. Clint filled his with Coco Puffs, then poured milk into each one.

Mom wandered into the kitchen from her bedroom. "Do you want to eat that in the living room?"

"Can we?" asked Clint.

"Sure. Let me help you."

She set up our little metal TV trays in the living room. They were just tall enough that we could sit on the floor, with the trays slid over our legs. Mine was blue and white with *Smurfs* on it. Clint's tray was adorned with G.I. Joes. Mom brought us our cereal, and Clint and I ate while watching reruns of *Captain Caveman* and *The Teen Angels* cartoon.

"Captain CAAAAAVEMAAAAAAANNNN!" we both shouted together several times throughout the show.

By 9:00 a.m., Clint and I had our fill of both cereal and cartoons for the day and were ready to do something else. We turned the TV off and went into our bedroom to change from pajamas to play clothes. It was getting close to winter, so it was too cold, foggy, and dreary to play outside. We would need to spend the day in the house.

"What do you want to do now, Clint?"

"Hmmm…do you want to watch the View-Master?"

I nodded. "Yes."

Clint found the square blue plastic box with a green dial and a long white cord attached to it. It was the View-Master Theatre Projector. He took it into Cody's nursery and set it up just right so that the projector would show the pictures on the wall. I looked all around our bedroom and finally found the little red box that had all of our View-Master slides in it. They were round cardboard disks that had small square images on them.

I carried the box of slides into Cody's bedroom, set them next to Clint and the projector, then went to find Mom. She was in the laundry room holding Cody while she took a load of clothes out of the dryer.

I took hold of one of Cody's feet. "Mom, can Cody watch View-Master with us?" I sometimes wished I were big enough to hold him all by myself.

"Of course, but I doubt he'll sit still long enough. Can you and Clint help with cleaning the house first?"

Cody was never good at staying in one spot for too long; now that he could walk, he was always on the move.

"Okay, let me tell Clint." I ran through the house shouting, "Clint!"

"What?"

"We have to help with cleaning the house."

"Okay."

Mom asked us, "What do you want to help with today? You can each choose one."

"I'll vacuum." I actually took great joy in pushing our big red and white upright vacuum all through the house. The bright light on the front of it felt like I was driving a special car through the grass as I pushed the big vacuum over our dark green carpet.

"I guess I'll help fold the clothes," Clint said with not much enthusiasm.

We spent the next thirty minutes helping with housework. Clint helped Mom with the laundry, Dad did the dishes and cleaned the kitchen, and I pushed the vacuum all through the house. I'm not sure how much cleaning I actually did with the vacuum, but regardless, I had fun pushing it around, and I thought I was helping.

After the chores were done, my dad turned on the TV to watch college football. Mom followed Clint and me into Cody's bedroom and encouraged Cody to sit with us for a little while. She positioned him just right so that he could watch the View-Master slides. Then, Mom helped Clint put up the projector screen. She turned off the light and told us to have fun when she left the room.

Clint, Cody, and I huddled together on the floor in the dark. Clint pushed the projector button for each new picture. We watched the pictures, and Clint and I explained each one to Cody who watched with wide eyes. We had pictures of everything from zoo animals to Star Wars characters. The longer we sat there, the more animated we got in telling stories to go with each picture.

"Touchdown!" Dad shouted from the living room. His favorite college football team had just scored.

Clint and I went to the living room to see what the score was. Cody ran ahead of us and tripped in the process, so he started to cry. Dad picked Cody up to console him, and Clint and I tried to decide what we wanted to do with the rest of our day.

I sighed. "Well, I'm hungry."

"Me, too." Dad agreed. "Let's eat lunch."

We went to the kitchen, where Mom had already started making tuna sandwiches. Dad helped her as much as he could while still holding Cody. Clint and I got some off-brand barbecue potato chips out of the cupboard and pickles out of the fridge. We sat at the breakfast bar, and Mom passed us the sandwiches on white paper plates.

"These look great, Boop," said Dad. Even though her name was Betty, he always called her Boop. There's a certain story behind her nickname that always makes me laugh.

The story goes like this: Mom and Dad were at a friend's house, and some people that my parents had never met were also there. That whole night, my dad kept referring to my mom as "Boop," like he always did. He didn't know a newcomer in the group had been offended by Dad's nickname for Mom. It took my dad the whole night to figure out why, then everyone had a good laugh when he finally discovered that the new friend thought Dad was calling my mom "Boobs" not "Boop." After that night, my parents' friends would sometimes refer to my mom as "Boobs" just for fun.

After all the sandwiches were passed out, I realized that Clint's plate didn't have a tuna sandwich. "What kind of sandwich is Clint eating?"

"It's bologna, mustard, and ketchup," said Mom.

"Eew, gross!"

"It's the only thing he'll eat right now, so that's what he's getting."

Clint laughed. "I like it! Do you want a bite?" He held his sandwich close to my face.

I pushed it away. "Yuck! No!"

When we finished eating lunch, Mom held up a small brown pill bottle. "It's time for your medicine, Clint."

He stayed in the kitchen, and I went in the living room. I stood next to the gold rocking chair for a few minutes, watching my adorable little brother sleep in Dad's arms.

Clint always took a while to take his medicine, and he never felt very good afterward, so I knew that my play time with him was over for now. I stood close to Dad for a few minutes oohing and aahing over Cody, when something caught my eye. It was Clint's tall, gray plastic mountain, sitting next to the wall in the dining room looking a little out of place.

Clint used the mountain for his little green army men, his *Star Wars* and G.I. Joe action figures. I was sure that he wouldn't mind me playing without him.

Beeeeeeep.

Just then, Dad's red fire pager went off and could be heard throughout the house.

Dad jumped up from the rocking chair and headed toward the kitchen. Like a football, he handed Cody off to Mom, who was still helping Clint with his medicine.

The pager was loud enough for all of us to hear, and we listened closely to what was being announced over the scanner. The dispatcher was still talking when Dad quickly grabbed his bulky yellow fire gear and put it on over his clothes. It sounded like he was being called to an accident on Highway 99.

"When are they ever going to get rid of that dumb stoplight?" Mom asked to nobody in particular.

Dad shook his head. "I don't know, Boop, but I sure hope there aren't any fatalities. With this fog, it's probably a bad accident."

After Dad had everything he needed for the fire call, he gave Mom a kiss goodbye. He ruffled Clint's and my hair, we knew that was his reminder that he loved us. He put on his yellow hard plastic fire helmet and hurried out the door. "Be good!" he called over his shoulder.

Later in my life I came to understand that when my dad said, "Be good," he didn't mean it as just a reminder to stay out of trouble, but also to be happy, joyful, to love each other, and to do good. There were so many emotions wrapped up in those two words. He really did always want us to just *be good*.

"When are they ever going to fix that stoplight?" Mom sounded frustrated.

I looked at her. "What stoplight?"

Clint reminded me. "You know, the one on the highway. The one by Foster Farms."

"Oh. What's wrong with it?"

"It shouldn't be there," said Mom. "It's so dangerous."

"Why?" I did not understand why it was such an issue.

"Because on Highway 99, people drive really fast, and they aren't expecting to have to stop. It's the only stoplight on Highway 99 from Sacramento all the way to Mexico."

Clint and I both said, "Mexico?"

"Well, something like that." Mom seemed to question her own statement. "In this thick fog, people can't see the light until they're right up on it, and by then it's usually too late. I just hope everyone's okay. That light scares me," she started to trail off as she looked out the kitchen window. "Your dad will help them, though. He and the other volunteer firefighters will do what they're trained to do."

Many years later, and after many more accidents, the stoplight on Highway 99 was removed. In 1997, the highway was rebuilt as a modern-day freeway to help prevent any further accidents. It was a joyful sight for most but also brought on a bit of sadness as it was the end of an era. A sign of the increase in population and modernization.

Clint yawned. "I'm tired."

Mom encouraged him. "You should go lie down."

Clint went to our bedroom, and I trailed behind him to find some things to play with. I hadn't forgotten about the gray plastic mountain, and I needed just the right toys to make it come alive. Mom followed close behind us to put Cody down for a nap. Then she took a book to the family room and sat in her favorite spot to read.

I was busy looking in our closet to find what I needed. First, I found the brown cardboard box full of Clint's army men, then some G.I. Joe action figures, a few of my Barbies, some plastic Fisher Price people, the little plastic farm animals, and the little brown plastic fences for the animals. I put them all in the box with the army men. I carried them into the living room and spent the rest of the day building a little city with Clint's and my toys. I strategically placed the little men high up on the mountain to keep watch over my little city as the Barbies and Fisher Price people took care of the farm animals and played with each other. Mom poked her head into the living room; I think to make sure I was still content.

A good chunk of the day had disappeared when I heard Mom walk up behind me. "Do you want to help me make dinner?"

"Yep, what are we having?"

"Scalloped potatoes, green beans, and ham."

"Yum."

"Okay, let me help you pick up your toys, and then we can get to slicing the potatoes."

Mom quickly helped me put all of the toys back in our bedroom, and she checked on Clint. He was still asleep, but I was sure he'd be up soon. She went to Cody's room to wake him up from his nap. He was always starving when he woke up, so she put him in his high chair and gave him something to snack on while we made dinner.

Soon, dinner was ready, and Clint was awake. We all got settled at the breakfast bar, eating our supper together, wishing that Dad could be with us. We said a prayer for those involved in the accident on 99 and hoped that everyone was okay. Dad had been gone for several hours, so we knew that the worst-case scenario was probably what had him and the other firefighters taking so long to get home. Mom had been listening to updates on the scanner but kept the details of the updates to herself.

We ate dinner rather quickly, then cleaned up, and Mom popped popcorn in our big orange dome electric corn popper. We watched the kernels go round and round, being pushed by the silver metal rod in the middle of the popper; we waited patiently for the kernels to heat up and start popping.

We talked about the time when Mom was popping popcorn and the power went out. It was a rainy afternoon with lots of thunderstorms. When she plugged the popper into the wall, the power went out. She thought she had blown a circuit or something, so she quickly unplugged the popper, and the power came back on.

We all laughed at the crazy coincidence, then Mom went to check the breakers. Everything was fine, so she decided to try plugging it in again. As soon as she did, the power went out again. She quickly unplugged it, saying she hoped that she hadn't done any permanent damage, but the power didn't come back on. Instead, it was out for the rest of the night. After telling my grandparents the story, everyone blamed Mom and the popcorn popper for the power outage that day.

Finally, the popcorn was finished, and Mom flipped the popper over so that the big orange dome became our popcorn bowl. We carried it into the living room, where we all watched a VHS movie together on our TV using our new VCR.

After the movie was over, it was time for bed. Dad got home sometime in the middle of the night and came into our bedroom to tell both Clint and me that he had made it home safely. He kissed us both. He had been gone for a long time, and I could hear the exhaustion in his voice. I wondered if anyone had died in the accident, but I didn't really want to know the answer to that question, so I didn't ask.

At the Livingston Firehouse 1983. Larry Perreira working on the fire engine while Dad (Gene) and I watch closely.

SUNDAY

Watching football together helped us forget about the realities of life.

~KIMBERLEY'S THOUGHT~

THE SMELL OF SAUSAGE cooking woke me from a deep sleep. The aroma of maple and spices made my stomach grumble; it was time for breakfast.

"Clint, are you awake?" I quietly asked.

He didn't answer me, so I rolled out from under the warmth of my comforter and climbed up on the wooden ladder just enough to peek and see if he was there. To my surprise, he wasn't. I climbed back down and walked into the living room, where Clint was sitting on the couch. He was looking at a book with pieces of toilet paper shoved up each nostril of his nose. He must have been woken up by a bloody nose sometime in the middle of the night.

"Do you want hot chocolate?" I remembered that I wasn't only hungry, but I was cold and thirsty, too. The heater was working hard to bring the temperature inside the house up as much as it could on that fall morning; however, it didn't quite reach the level of warmth that I preferred.

Clint nodded. "Sure."

I went to the kitchen to see who was cooking sausage and to ask whichever parent it was if Clint and I could have hot chocolate.

Mom was chipper. "Good morning, sleepy head."

"Good morning. Can we have hot chocolate?" I already knew the answer was yes because we always had hot chocolate with breakfast if we were home on Sunday mornings. Nevertheless, I wasn't big enough to make it by myself, so I had to ask for it.

"Of course." Mom turned the sausage.

I climbed up onto the brown leather cushioned barstool at the breakfast bar and watched her mix all the ingredients into a bowl for French toast. She put a piece of bread into the bowl to soak while she got everything that she needed for the hot chocolate, including miniature marshmallows.

"I want my Swiss Miss mug," I reminded her.

"I know. With that blonde hair of yours, Swiss Miss looks just like you."

The smile on my face showed that I agreed with her.

"Do you want me to braid your hair for church today?"

I nodded. "Yes."

"Okay, I'll do it right after we eat."

Mom helped me make two mugs of hot chocolate, then she went back to making the French toast. I climbed off the barstool and went into the living room to let Clint know that his hot chocolate was ready. He followed me back into the kitchen, where we both sat at the breakfast bar and quietly drank our hot treat while Mom finished making breakfast.

Mom asked Clint. "Is your nose still bleeding?"

"I don't think so." He removed the pieces of toilet paper from his nostrils. He threw them in the trash and went to the bathroom to wash his hands. In no time at all, he was sitting next to me again.

I was happy to see that his nose had stopped bleeding. One,

because nobody wants a bloody nose, and two, because I secretly hated seeing bloody pieces of toilet paper or tissue sticking out of his nose. Seeing that always reminded me that he was sick, and I really didn't want him to be sick anymore.

Mom and Dad's bedroom was right off the family room, which opened up into the kitchen. The breakfast bar served as a sort of barrier between the family room and kitchen. Dad would have to walk past all of us to get to Cody's bedroom at the opposite end of the house.

"Good morning, Clinto, good morning, Pumpkin, breakfast smells scrumptious, Boop!" he ruffled Clint's and my hair on his way to Cody's nursery. It was nice to see that Dad had gotten some sleep after getting home so late from his fire call last night.

The next hour was filled with us enjoying breakfast together. It was a meal that even Clint ate because he was able to smother his French toast in powdered sugar and strawberries. After we finished and the kitchen was cleaned up, I sat on the barstool while Mom braided my hair.

It was time to get ready for church, and we each went in our own directions to get dressed in our Sunday best. I knew Mom would spritz her wrists and neck with perfume, and Dad would put on what he called his "smelly good stuff" or "Col-og-knee." It was usually a splash of Old Spice or Stetson cologne.

We dashed out the door, climbed into our blue Toyota Corolla, and headed to town.

It wasn't foggy that morning, so it didn't take us long to make the drive from our house to the main part of Livingston, where we attended church. As we drove into town, we passed by "The House with Nobody In It," the Pink Store, the high school, the Candy Cane house, the park, and then I saw the big wooden cross and two big palm trees on the left-hand side of the street; we had made it to church.

The palm trees on Main Street had a story behind them that always sparked my curiosity. They looked so out of place in our town, being so far away from the ocean. The house that once stood there was said to have been the place where the notorious Dalton Gang used to hide out.

"That's where the Dalton Gang hid out," Mom would often say when we drove past the palm trees. She'd sometimes tell us the story that she'd heard over the years about how one of the brothers in the Dalton Gang fell in love with the daughter who lived there, and that they eventually got married. There is debate about that story from some historians, but I've always believed it to be true because it's the same story that Grandma Pierce would tell me as well, and who doesn't love a good love story?

Other times when we drove passed the palm trees, Mom would tell us about how the mansion that once stood there was haunted. She'd go into detail about how it looked inside and how there were rats in the walls. She and her dad, my grandpa, walked all around it before they tore it down in the late 1950s. A memory she treasures. The Baptist church was built on the land where the house once stood, which is something my grandpa was always bitter about. It bothered him that they tore the old house down that was filled with so much history to the town to, "Build a dumb church."

Ironically, that *dumb church* was the Baptist church that we began going to a few years before Cody was born. My parents were strong believers in God but weren't huge fans of organized religion. Once they were married, they had never really planned on attending any church. In addition to that, they had lived in remote places where Dad was a park ranger, and going to church hadn't really been an option for them until moving to Livingston. It wasn't until the miracle occurred with Clint surviving a terrible head injury in 1980 that their thoughts changed about Christianity and attending a church. It only takes the blink of an eye for someone's whole world and whole perspective on life to shift.

The story goes like this…

My parents had taken Clint and me to the drive-in movies in Modesto to see the movie, *101 Dalmatians*. Clint and I were playing on the playground waiting for the movie to start. I was only two years old at the time, so my parents were keeping a close eye on me while Clint played on the metal monkey bars. He suddenly slipped and hit his head really hard on the metal steps of the play set. He cracked his head open, was knocked unconscious, and went into convulsions.

Dad scooped him up and quickly got him in the car, and Mom carried me. They rushed him to the closest hospital. It didn't take long for doctors to determine that Clint had two blood clots on his brain. He suffered both a subdural and epidural hematoma and wasn't expected to survive the night. My parents were told that if by some miracle he did survive and regain consciousness, he would have permanent brain damage and would be a vegetable, someone who is typically in a vegetative state and lacks awareness and cognitive function due to severe brain damage, likely for the rest of his life.

Again, we were in the hospital with Clint. For years, he had been fighting for his life, battling leukemia, and now they were told to say their final goodbyes as doctors explained how they would try to relieve the pressure from Clint's brain. My parents watched Clint looking lifeless on his bed as he was rushed in for emergency surgery. They have said they felt helpless, trying to grapple with the idea of him becoming a vegetable. Or even worse, perhaps not ever seeing him alive again. They leaned on each other for hope and prayed for a miracle.

Doctors cut a piece of Clint's skull to relieve pressure and placed a metal plate in his head. When the surgery was over, Clint was taken to the intensive care unit, where he was closely monitored. The doctors told everyone that it would be at least five days before Clint would wake up, if ever at all. Four hours after the surgery, my parents returned to the intensive care unit, with me in their arms, to find the nurses in a state of shock. Not only was Clint awake, but he was talking! The nurses who were closely monitoring him couldn't believe their ears when he muttered the words, "Where's my TV?" He had been in many hospital rooms in his young life and usually always had a TV, so he was a bit confused as to why that room didn't have one.

"Hi, Mom. Hi, Dad. I love you," Clint said as everyone within earshot started to cry. It wasn't until years later that I learned more about what took place that day. A miracle that my family has talked about many times over the years. Many believe it is just a story because it seems so truly unbelievable, but my brother, Clint, is living proof that a miracle really did occur that day, and he was always proud to share his story with anyone who would listen.

Since that miracle, my parents felt it was important for all of us kids to learn about the Bible and to be exposed to the stories that were in it. So, we were all sitting in Sunday school learning about the teachings of Jesus and singing hymns while my parents attended the regular church service with the adults. My parents still didn't wholeheartedly believe in organized religion, but going to church helped with their search for explanations about the miracle that took place, and it was also an outlet for them to express their frustrations about Clint's continuing battle with cancer. Church was a place where my parents gave thanks for the miracle that took place while encouraging others, as well as our family, to continue to have hope. Talking the miracle over with the pastor and studying the Bible helped them to embrace what was, and come to the realization that God is everywhere, not just in church.

After the service, we drove back to our house to enjoy the rest of the day as a family. As soon as we got home, we all changed into our play clothes, and Dad turned on the TV for us to watch Sunday football. He was thrilled that the game was his favorite team, the 49ers. We ate sandwiches for lunch while we gathered in the living room to watch them play the Atlanta Falcons. All of us except Clint rooted for the 49ers to win.

It was then that I learned Clint was a Kansas City Chiefs fan.

Thinking that I needed to have a different favorite football team, too, I asked my dad, "How do you decide what your favorite football team is?"

"Well," he said, "everyone chooses their favorite teams differently. Some people choose their favorite teams based on where they live. For example, I root for the San Francisco 49ers because I was born and raised in San Francisco."

"But Clint wasn't born and raised in Kansas City."

"That's true. Some people also choose their favorite teams by their favorite colors or their favorite mascots."

"That makes sense."

"What is your favorite color?"

"Blue."

"Okay, so let's think about the football teams that have blue uniforms."

He named off all those football teams with that color. There were so many that I couldn't decide.

He then asked, "What is your favorite animal?"

"Dogs."

He laughed. "Well, there aren't many NFL teams that have a dog as their mascot. What's another favorite animal?"

"I like horses."

"Okay, then you might like the Colts. Their mascot is a colt, which is a baby male horse. And their jerseys are blue and white. You might also like the Cowboys, they ride horses, and the Cowboys' football team uniforms are blue, silver, and white."

"Okay, my favorite teams are the Colts and the Cowboys," I said proudly, determined to like a different team other than the 49ers.

"You can have lots of favorite teams. You can still like the 49ers, too, if you want," Dad reminded me.

I smiled. "Okay, the 49ers are my favorite, too." I knew that my liking the same team that he did would make him happy.

"You can also like a certain team because of their players," said Mom.

"What are your favorite teams?" I asked her.

"The Jets and the Patriots."

"Why?"

"When I was a sophomore in high school, I liked their quarterbacks. It drove my dad crazy, so being the rebel that I was, I grew to like both of those teams even more," Mom said with pride.

"So, we all have different favorite teams." I realized, not sure if I liked that or not.

"We do." Mom agreed, "But we all like football, and it can be fun to root for different teams."

We finished watching the rest of the game as Dad explained some of the rules to me. Even though I'd been watching football my whole life, I was only five, and there were still some rules that I didn't quite understand. Dad was animated in explaining certain plays to me as he reminisced about what it was like to be a player on a football field.

Since I'd determined that the 49ers were now one of my favorite teams, I sat with Dad rooting for them to win. It was a close game that came right down to the wire. Unfortunately, the Falcons pulled off the win. There was a certain feeling that arose inside of me, experiencing what it's like to have your favorite team lose. A part of me wanted to cry because I was sad that my team lost, but a part of me was also a little bit mad at the other team for winning.

Dad seemed to understand my frustration and changed the focus to something else. "Let's play football."

"In the house?" Mom scowled.

Dad laughed. "Don't worry, we'll be careful this time. I'll even play on my knees."

Mom sighed. "I'm leaving. I don't want to watch anything get broken. I'll be in the family room reading a book."

We'd played football in the house many times before, and it usually always ended in either someone getting hurt or something getting broken, but that didn't stop us.

We determined that the teams would be Clint and I against Cody and Dad. Cody was just a little over a year old, so Clint and I saw him as no threat. We could certainly win the game, especially if Dad was willing to play on his knees. Clint went into our room to get his little blue Nerf football and his red striped plastic football helmet that used to be Dad's when he was a little boy. He came back into the living room holding the ball and put the helmet on.

I knew he was reminding me that he was going to be the quarterback first.

Clint and I huddled up to determine our route as Dad and Cody did the same. With that, the game started. Clint tossed me the ball, and I ran toward where the predetermined end zone was in the living room, but before I could get in to make a touchdown, Dad gently tackled me to the ground, pretending to be tackling me with full force. The game went on with me running, then Cody running, then Dad running on his knees, then me being the quarterback, and Clint running.

As the game went on, we got more into it and soon forgot that we were in the house. Dad tried to gently throw Cody a pass, but it bounced off Clint's helmet and flew into the air in the direction of the bronze-colored cowboy lamp that was sitting on the end table by the gold chair.

Crash!

The sound reverberated throughout the house as the football flew into the lamp.

"I heard that!" Mom hollered from the family room.

"It's okay, it's not broken." Dad laughed while quickly inspecting the lamp to ensure that it wasn't. "Okay, kids, I guess that's game over."

The rest of our Sunday was spent with each of us doing our own thing. Mom spent some time reading, and Dad went into the family room to play his guitar. Clint was pretty worn out from the football game, so he relaxed on the floor playing with his Lincoln Logs and Brick Blocks, teaching Cody how to carefully stack them up to create things instead of putting them in his mouth.

It was then that I realized Clint looked larger, different, balder, and sicker. I could tell he didn't feel good, but he seemed to be happy to be home for a few days, so that made all the difference.

I went into the family room and practiced twirling my baton. While she read, Mom watched a little. Then she put her book down and tried to teach me new ways to twirl the baton without hitting the pool table. She got her own baton out of the closet, then spent a lot of time demonstrating how she used to twirl it like the majorettes did when she was in high school. I watched in awe at how magical it looked when she'd toss it in the air and catch it so flawlessly. I tried repeatedly to do the same thing but just went back to twirling because that was easier.

After I got bored with that, I ran off to my bedroom to get my black Lone Ranger mask. I loved pretending to be the Lone Ranger whenever the opportunity arose. I went all through the house, shooting at things with my cap gun that weren't actually there. The *pop* sound of the gun startled me every time I pulled the trigger, but I loved the burnt sulfur smell that steamed off each shot.

Soon it was time for dinner, showers, and bedtime. Our Sunday was over, but we were all thankful for the day that we were able to spend together. It was really nice when we were all in the house at the same time. It didn't happen very often in those years with Clint being so sick. Someone was usually away with him at the doctor's or the hospital while I stayed with my cousin, grandparents, or family friends. Also, Dad was often away on fire calls or busy helping Papa with something on the ranch, so his absence was noticed as well. Time to just be together was our favorite thing.

Playing football in the house 1983.
Cody and Clint getting ready to score a touchdown.

THANKSGIVING

Being thankful is so much more than just saying grace.
~KIMBERLEY'S THOUGHT~

OUR WHOLE FAMILY stood in the middle of the street, surrounded by cold fog. We could barely see the almond trees in the field next to us, but we knew they were there. We had ski caps on our heads and were wearing our warmest jackets as we determined who would get the ball first. My dad, Clint, and I huddled up to decide the play and who would catch the football next; my cousins did the same for their team. After we'd determined our play, I crouched down to get ready to hike the ball between my legs.

Dad called, "Blue forty-two, hut, hut, hike!"

I hiked the ball. He caught it and threw it right into Clint's arms just like we had planned.

"Run, run!" he called as Clint made it past the point that we had marked as the goal line.

"Touchdown!" Clint raised both arms in the air.

It was nice to see that he was feeling well enough to make a touchdown.

After several days of back-and-forth trips to the hospital, our family was reunited as one just in time for Thanksgiving. With the help of medication and close monitoring by my parents, Clint was able to stay home for a while. His body looked different. He was larger and all puffed up because of the prednisone he was taking, but he still acted the same. He was losing his hair *again* because of the radiation and chemotherapy, but he didn't seem to mind. He was just happy to be home, and we embraced every moment that we were all able to be together.

It was tradition for the family to play football in the street every Thanksgiving while the food was cooking, and that year was no exception. The teams were a little different each year, depending on who wanted to play and who in the extended family was able to make it to my grandparents' house for the holiday. I don't remember which team ever won. It was just a matter of practicing catching and throwing the football while having fun.

After we'd had our fill of playing football, it was time to head inside my grandparents' house for a snack. We could smell the turkey and stuffing cooking in the oven as we walked across their front lawn with leaves crunching under our feet. The aroma of the Thanksgiving feast filled the air. We could all hear our stomachs growling as we waited for the tasty meal to finish cooking.

As soon as we got inside, Papa made each of us kids a Shirley Temple while we grabbed cheese and crackers from the kitchen table to put on our paper plates. We gathered in the living room in front of the TV set to watch the end of the Macy's Thanksgiving Day Parade. All of us kids waited patiently to watch Santa Claus appear on the screen to signify the end of the parade. We watched in awe as Santa waved to the onlookers, sure that he was looking right at us.

We scarfed down our cheese and crackers and waited to see what was coming up next on TV. We watched the kickoff of the first football game of the day while the food finished cooking. Thanksgiving for our family always consisted of food and football, so that's all we had on our minds. We all cheered for our favorite teams, and if ours weren't playing, then we'd cheer for our favorite players.

Most of the grown-ups stayed in the living room watching the game while a few of us wandered into the kitchen to see if our feast was almost done. We breathed in the warm, turkey-smelling air as our Papa opened the oven to check the temperature of the bird. It was so close. We offered our help in getting ready for the Thanksgiving feast.

Dad, Papa, and my uncles carried in two long rectangular fold-out tables from the garage and a card table from the office. They then made another trip outside to gather the folding chairs. Once in the house, they set them all up in the living room but out of the way of the football game. They also carried chairs in from the kitchen to fill in the extra spots.

My cousins and I helped spread each of the tables with white tablecloths that were covered in fall-colored turkeys and leaves. The square table was special just for us kids. Clint rested in my grandma's chair, watching the football game and watching us all, probably wishing that he felt well enough to help.

After the tables were covered, my cousin Kerry and I helped Grandma set forks, spoons, knives, the good China plates, and paper napkins in just the right spots. Ensuring that everyone would have the same setup, we double checked each other's work as we moved along to the next place setting. We then set out the good crystal wine glasses placing them at the top of each plate. Even the kids' place settings had a wine glass. It was tradition for everyone to have at least a sip of our grandparents' wine after we clanked our glasses together in a cheer before taking our first bite of Thanksgiving dinner. My cousin and I always opted for a sip of white wine while many of the grown-ups opted for red.

After tables were completely set, Kerry and I carefully helped Grandma, Mom, and my aunts set out some of the food. The banana pudding, candied yams, mashed potatoes, my great-grandpa's homemade green olives, canned pitted black olives, pickled baby corn, my grandma's homemade turkey stuffing, the homemade bubbling turkey gravy, green beans, corn, and the canned cranberry sauce were all placed in their proper spots. Clint wandered over to see if anything looked good for him to eat. He zeroed in on the mashed potatoes, claiming that he'd be the first one to scoop those onto his plate. Kerry and I laughed and then took turns sitting in different seats around the table. We tried to decide which seat was the best spot to have access to all our favorite foods.

We decided that the spots right in front of the olives were the best seats. We pretended to be grown-ups for a few minutes, knowing that we'd soon be kicked out of those spots by someone else in the family once dinner was ready to be served. We couldn't resist having an olive or two before everyone else was called to the table, so we reached into the clear, beautifully etched crystal bowl that held the pitted black olives. We put an olive on each of our fingers and wiggled them all about, laughing at how funny they felt before we ate them one by one.

"Turkey's done!" Papa called from the kitchen.

Kerry and I ran in to watch him take the large twenty-pound turkey out of the oven. It was glossy, brown, and swimming in a large metal pan of delicious-smelling turkey juices. We scooted out of his way as he placed the turkey on the bar in their kitchen. He carefully transferred the cooked bird from its large metal pan to the colorfully adorned platter that was used each year only on Thanksgiving. Papa then methodically scooped all the stuffing out of the turkey's body and placed it in a large white bowl with green flowers on it, that Grandma had set close by.

By that time, everyone in the family had crowded into the kitchen and waited patiently for Papa to start carving the turkey. "Is anyone hungry?" he joked.

"Yes!" we all laughed and shouted.

"Just checkin'." He held the carving knife in his right hand and the large fork to hold the turkey in place with his other hand. We all watched him make the first cut as the large slice of white turkey breast fell onto the platter.

"That looks good enough to eat!" Dad hollered, and we all laughed.

Papa slowly carved the rest of the turkey, ensuring that each slice was not too big and not too small but just right for each of us. As he continued cutting, he told all of us to go and find our seats at the table. We first all checked the score of the football game. All of us kids ran straight to our table that was placed right at the end of the grown-ups. We had our own little bowls of green and black olives. We would have to wait for the rest of the food to be shared with us after the grown-ups had dished up their own plates.

The head of the table was saved for Papa, and Grandma took the seat that was closest to his. The rest of the grown-ups found their own seats and admired how beautifully the table had been set. Kerry and I beamed, knowing that we had done our jobs well. Dad poured a little sip of wine into each of the kids' glasses, including mine, and someone added a few cubes of ice into our glasses to help tone down the wine a bit. Once everyone had some, we knew that it was almost time to eat.

"Gene, do you want to say something?" Papa asked, knowing that indeed he did. My dad was never short on words.

"Sure." Dad proceeded to say grace. "Lord, thank you for this food that is set before us, this great family, the doctors that are continuing to work hard to help Clint, for allowing Clint to be here with us instead of in the hospital, for all of our friends that continue to help us so much, and for my wonderful kids and wife who continue to put up with me. Amen. Now let's eat."

"Cheers!" We all hollered as we held up our wine in unison, clanking glasses with whoever was sitting closest. All of us kids took a sip of our white wine, scrunching up our faces pretending to like it before quickly taking a drink of our Shirley Temples to help wash it down. The grown-ups then passed the food down to our table so that we could dish up.

Clint piled his plate with mashed potatoes and corn while the rest of us took a little bit of everything. We all ate, talked, laughed, and shared stories until we were full to the gills. We stared at our plates, wondering if we could possibly put another bite into our mouths. The adults talked about how they'd have to unbutton their pants and be hauled away in wheelbarrows while the kids laughed and talked about dessert.

Grandma groaned. "Ugh…dessert? How could you possibly be ready for that?"

Everyone began cleaning off the table and putting things away. Dishes were taken into the kitchen to be washed, the leftover food was put in containers and stored in the fridge, the tables were carefully taken down and placed back where they had been stored, the chairs were all put back in the usual spots, and the house was restored to normal.

After the feast was over, we were spread throughout the house talking, playing, and watching football. At one point, all of us kids took turns playing on Grandma's Vita Master Weight Loss Shaker Massage Belt Machine in her bedroom. It was supposed to help her lose weight, but all of us kids just thought it was a big toy. We took turns standing on the machine's platform with the belt around our waist, then we flipped the switch on. It shook our bodies until we couldn't take it anymore and begged someone to turn it off. Nobody seemed to worry about us getting hurt, so we played with it until we got bored and ran off to find a game to play.

After we'd eaten a piece of pumpkin pie, and the last football game of the day was almost over, it was time to go home. My aunts Linda and Londa, our uncles, and cousins got in their cars to head for home in the neighboring town of Delhi. Our family made the short walk back to our house that was right there on the ranch.

Clint was exhausted from such a busy day, so Dad carried him and Mom carried Cody. I held Mom's hand as I walked solemnly, pressing my feet in the soft dirt.

I was sad that Thanksgiving was over and wondered when we'd all be together like that again. The part that always bothered me the most about those special days was that they always had to come to an end.

Papa and Grandma at their house getting ready to carve the turkey. Thanksgiving 1980 something.

PREPARING FOR CHRISTMAS

~KIMBERLEY'S THOUGHT~

THANKSGIVING CAME AND WENT like a thief in the night. The days that followed were dark, cold, and dreary. The persimmon trees were drooping with sadness as the last of their leaves fell to the ground in a messy heap on my grandparents' front lawn. The grapevines no longer held their big green leaves like they had the rest of the year, and the last of the grapes, trying their hardest to hang on, had shriveled up and fallen to the ground. All that surrounded our house now were bare vines that carefully wrapped their way around the wires that seemed to stretch for miles. The fog that often settled into the valley had been pushed out by a light, drizzly, winter rain that covered the grass with little droplets of water.

I was standing on our green leather couch looking out the window, off in my own little world. I watched the raindrops slowly sliding down the glass wondering how long it would be before we could go outside and play again. Not yet fully understanding the concept of time, I also wondered how long it would be before I'd be going back to school. Would I need to walk in this rain to the bus stop?

As my mind wandered, the energy in the living room shifted from calm to vibrant when Dad walked in.

"Who's ready to go get a Christmas tree?"

"Me!" I shouted.

"For real?" Clint asked. "But it's raining."

"That's okay, we'll put on our coats."

Mom came in from the kitchen. "It's just drizzly out, and it will be an adventure."

"Yay! Let's go!" I jumped down from the couch and ran into our bedroom to find my tennis shoes.

"Where will we get it?" asked Clint.

"The Christmas tree farm where Kim went for her kindergarten field trip," said Dad.

"We are?" I hobbled out of our bedroom, wearing both tennis shoes, with neither of them tied.

"Yes," said Mom. "They have beautiful trees."

Before I knew it, we were parked on the dirt at the Christmas tree farm that was only about twenty minutes from our house. We all jumped out of the car like it was on fire, and we quickly helped Cody out of his car seat. We were so excited to find a tree that none of us even seemed to notice the light drizzle still slowly falling from the sky.

We walked through the magnificent pines, and it didn't take us any time at all to pick out the perfect tree. We each took turns sawing at the trunk with the long-handled, green saw that the farm let us borrow.

We all shouted, "Timber!" as the tree fell to the ground with a soft thud.

Dad dragged the tree through the dirt until we reached our car. He paid the nice lady running the farm, then he and Mom strapped it to the roof of the car with white rope. Once they felt it was secure enough, we were on our way.

When we got home, I helped Cody out of his car seat, and Clint ran ahead to open the sliding glass door. Mom and Dad carefully removed the tree from the roof of the car and carried it into the house. The next hour was spent moving furniture and positioning the tree just right in front of the living room window. Getting it in the stand was always more of a chore than fun. Mom poured water into the tree stand along with an aspirin tablet. She said it was to help keep the tree fresh longer. Once it was in place, we admired the tree with anticipation of decorating it.

Mom and Dad brought the large cardboard box marked *Christmas* into the family room and set it on the pool table. We all gathered around as Mom removed the contents and spread them out. She pulled out Christmas lights; paper and plastic wall decorations; sparkly red, green, silver, and gold garland; Christmas ornaments; our stockings; and more.

Our favorite decorations were resting comfortably at the bottom of the box; the very colorful, melted popcorn-looking reindeer and matching Santa. We oohed and aahed when Mom set them on the pool table. Clint and I took turns holding all the decorations and talked about where we should put them throughout the house.

Dad brought another box into the room. We stood around him while he opened it, and I was giddy at the sight of the contents.

"It's the fireplace!" I was thrilled.

This was the most amazing Christmas decoration of all. The thought of pretend heat coming out of that red and white striped cardboard cutout fireplace filled my whole body with anticipation. I couldn't wait to help Mom and Dad put the fake fireplace on the wall closest to Clint's and my bedroom. We would pretend its fake heat could keep us warmer at night. Our house didn't have a real fireplace, so this one we set up at Christmas time brought a certain type of heat into our house that made our cold mobile home feel warmer.

Mom would often say about it, "The power of believing it's real."

Our house was so cold in the wintertime that I spent many mornings taking the silver rectangle metal covers off the heater vents so I could dangle my feet inside the vent itself and try to capture every bit of warmth that I possibly could. Clint and I would sometimes try and share one of the vents, but the opening was too small for us to fit all four of our legs in it. Besides, on really cold days, he would hog too much of my heat. When it came to being warm, I was always determined enough to claim a vent of my own, directing him to find a different one somewhere else in the house. I claimed the one in the family room by the pool table as my own, because it put out the most heat.

My mind was pulled away from thinking about being warm when Mom carefully opened the small cardboard box marked, *Christmas Fragile*. In that box was the Christmas village. Clint and I carefully took turns pulling out the colorful cardboard houses, the little plastic reindeer, the fake snow, and the little dwarfs with round heads and pointy hats whose bodies were made of pinecones. We took the box over to my mom's cedar hope chest and laid the fake snow on top of it. Clint piled some of it up in a corner to make it look like a hill at the edge of the pretend village. We then methodically placed each tiny cardboard house in the perfect spot. Dad would later add small white lights to the village, which would make it come alive.

When we started decorating the house, Dad put on an Oakridge Boys record, and we hummed along to the music. We spent the next few hours moving about joyfully putting all the decorations in perfect spots, saving the tree for last. Dad put the tall red spire tree topper on first. The white light on the topper would soon serve as a beacon lighting the top of the tree. Mom and Dad helped each other wrap the colorful Christmas lights around the tree while Clint and I pulled out the ornaments. We carefully placed the ornaments on the tree as Dad wrapped silver garland on the branches. Last, we opened a new box of silver tinsel, and Mom showed us how to carefully place two or three strands at a time on the branches. Cody and Clint became frustrated and started just throwing tinsel in gobs. They then ran off into Cody's bedroom to play as Mom and I tried to clean up their tinsel mess. Dad strung the rest of the colorful garland throughout the whole house as Mom and I finished up the last of the tree decorating.

After all the garland was in place, Dad set up the cutout fireplace on the wall closest to mine, Clint, and Cody's bedrooms. He put all the pieces together like a jigsaw puzzle, ensuring that the fireplace stood upright without falling over. He connected the red light bulb to the center of the fireplace and attached the metal disk that swiveled on top of it so that it looked as if real flames were roaring in the fire. After it was completely in place, he hung each of our stockings on it. Each one had different pictures on the front, but they were all thick on top where Mom had written our names with glue and covered them with gold glitter. Our names shone brightly as the stockings dangled gently from the white fireplace mantle, anticipating Santa's arrival.

Once the house was fully decorated, Mom met with Clint and me, reminding us that we should start practicing for our Christmas Eve play. The play was a family tradition that started when she was a little girl. She read through a few Christmas poems that were in her green *Best Loved Poems of the American People* book to give us an idea of which poem we wanted to act out and make into a play. We finally settled on, "Willie and Annie's Prayer," by Sophia P. Snow.

We practiced our play for a few minutes before agreeing to practice it again another day.

In the days that followed, Clint and I began writing our letters to Santa. Clint's letter was short and to the point. He simply stated what he hoped Santa would bring him and signed his name at the bottom in a hurried swoop.

I, on the other hand, took days on my letter to Santa. For hours I mulled over the exact words I wanted to write, the perfect message I wanted to send, and the precise present that I thought only Santa could bring me. I started my letter by asking Santa about Rudolph, his other reindeer, and Mrs. Claus. I then asked, if it was possible, I'd love to have something special for my *big doll*.

After both of our letters were finally written, we put them in our stockings for Santa, or one of his helpers, to get while we were sleeping. The next morning, our letters were gone. I spent every day after that looking in my stocking to see if Santa had snuck something into it when nobody was looking. It was my own little tradition that I carried out throughout my entire childhood. It wasn't until my junior year of high school that I finally found something hiding in my stocking a week before Christmas. If only the world could have seen my excitement when I reached my hand into my stocking and found a VHS tape of *Little House on the Prairie, Christmas at Plum Creek.* I still don't know who put that special gift in my stocking, but I'm positive that it was someone who knew my heart and the joy that special surprise would bring me.

We started practicing our Christmas Eve play. The hours dragged into days with anticipation for Christmas to hurry up and get there. Waiting for the special day to arrive felt like torture with each passing day.

Mom kept telling me, "The joy is in the waiting."

Her comment made no sense to me at all at the time because I knew I would be full of joy when it was *finally* Christmas morning. Looking back now, I realize that Mom was right. The joy really was in the waiting. It's funny how time changes things.

Mom, me, Cody, and Clint decorating for Christmas 1983. Cody and Clint getting a little carried away with the tinsel.

14

SICK AT CHRISTMASTIME

~KIMBERLEY'S THOUGHT~

CHRISTMAS WAS DRAWING CLOSER, and no matter how hard we tried to forget about it, our family continued to be reminded of the battle that was going on in our lives. The thing about cancer and illness is that it doesn't stop for the holidays. Clint became sicker with each passing day, so trips to the hospital were more frequent than normal. For me to continue to go to school, I spent many days staying with Bill and Donna, my cousin Kerry, and my grandparents.

Mom, Dad, Clint, and Cody made countless trips together to and from the hospital. And almost every school day, I still received the daily question from the lunch card lady, "How is your brother doing?" I stayed with the safe answer of "fine" because it was just easier than going into any details about his condition.

It was just a week before Christmas, and since school was out for break, I was able to make the journey to the hospital with my family. My favorite of Clint's oncology doctor's small office was strewn with papers and books. Doctor Beach talked about how a bone marrow transplant might be the only hope for Clint's survival. It had been a few weeks since I'd been with Clint to see any of his doctors, so I tried hard to fully understand what she was talking about.

Each member of our family was tested, and doctors were astounded by the results. Cody was a perfect match for Clint, which was almost unheard of to find a match so quickly, so everyone was thrilled with that news. Mom and Dad were a perfect match for each other, which was great news if either of them ever needed a bone marrow transplant. I didn't match anybody, though, which left me feeling like an outsider. Certainly, I must be a match for someone? I stood in the hallway of Dr. Beach's office, wishing that I had my big doll with me to hold tight as I tried to grasp what was happening to our family. We'd left in such a hurry that morning that somehow, I'd left her behind.

To lighten the mood and ease tension, Mom took Cody and me into the oncology waiting room to look through *Highlight* magazines and books. As we were sitting there, I noticed a large box up against the wall filled with presents. I'd been in the oncology waiting room countless times before and had never seen a box like that.

I was curious. "Why are there presents in here?"

"I'm not sure. They must be for the patients." Mom was preoccupied trying to prevent Cody from eating the book that he was holding.

"Oh." My five-year-old mind did not fully understand the realities of life, so I wished I were a patient so that I could have one. I stood by the box just looking at all the beautifully wrapped presents.

A nurse wearing purple scrubs walked through the door. She looked at me and said, "Those Christmas presents are for everyone."

My eyes lit up with that news. She smiled and went back out.

"You can pick one out then," said Mom. She sounded tired.

She let Cody climb off her lap. "Cody can, too."

"Are you sure we can?" I was still unsure if the presents were truly for everyone.

"Go ahead. It's Christmas time, and the nurse said it's okay."

I suddenly felt guilty that I had wished to be sick so I could have one. "But should we save them for the patients?"

"No, it's okay. I'm sure there are some stored somewhere else for the patients. Since those are out here in the waiting room, those must be for everyone else." Mom sounded more relaxed.

My heart filled with joy as Cody and I carefully held up each present, trying to decide which one to pick. Cody chose a round one wrapped in green and red striped paper. He quickly opened it to reveal a small orange basketball that he immediately threw in my mom's direction. She must have anticipated his throw and caught it with no problem at all.

I finally settled on a present that was wrapped in shiny white and red paper. I took it over to a chair by Mom and carefully unwrapped it. Inside was a small black and white stuffed penguin wearing a green and red scarf.

"It's so cute." I held it close in my arms, gushing over the penguin that was now mine.

"That was really sweet of someone to bring presents for everyone," said Mom.

"It was. Should we pick one out for Clint?"

"Clint can pick one out when he's done visiting with the doctor."

That made sense.

Thankfully, on that visit, Clint didn't have to be hospitalized. We all left the hospital together, and Dad drove us to a Toys "R" Us store that was close by. It had been a long day filled with hard-to-hear news, so walking through the best toy store around was like taking a trip to the world's best amusement park.

"Now remember, before we go in there, we're just here to look and have fun," Dad reminded us kids.

"Clint's medicine and medical bills are very expensive, so we don't have the money to buy anything. Plus, Christmas will be here soon," Mom added.

"We know." Clint and I both nodded, eager to get inside the store just to look. We seldom ever got anything at that giant toy store, but looking and dreaming was just as much fun.

Cody looked wide-eyed at all of us, probably trying to understand why Clint and I were so excited to be parked in front of a building with a giraffe on the sign.

"Out." I knew he was anxious to get out of his car seat.

The next hour was spent walking up and down the aisles of Toy "R" Us, admiring the toys on the shelves, and holding some of them in our hands. Mom reminisced about some of the ones she had as a kid while Dad rode a bike down one of the aisles, and Clint tried to race him on a big trike. Cody looked mesmerized. His already big brown eyes widened as we showed him toy after toy. The stop had done us all good, and we left full of joy for our journey back to the ranch.

As Christmas drew closer, Mom and Dad kept us kids busy. I knew they were trying to take everyone's minds off the fact that Clint was very sick, and that it might very well have been our last Christmas together as a family. It wasn't something that we ever spoke about out loud, but it's something that we all knew was a possibility.

We spent the next few days looking through the Sears Christmas catalog over and over again, trying to decide what else we should have asked Santa for. We also spent time watching Christmas movies and cartoons on TV, playing with toys, coloring, and drawing pictures with crayons. The cold December days seemed to drag on as going outside and playing wasn't an option.

Mom announced early one morning, "Let's make some Christmas ornaments."

She had made salt dough from scratch and was excited to have us play with it. So, we all gathered around our card table that she set up in the living room and looked at the soft white dough in wonderment. We each tasted a little bite of the dough and quickly learned that it was way too salty to eat. She laughed and placed Christmas-shaped cookie cutters on the table. Each of us took turns pressing them into the dough. Even Cody pressed down on some of the cutters to help make shapes of teddy bears, candy canes, angels, and the like. After all the dough was cut into shapes, Mom used a straw to press a small hole into the top of each ornament, then she put them in the oven to cook.

Mom left the oven light on for us so that Clint and I could take turns looking through the glass, to check on the ornaments to ensure that they were cooking. Once they were done, we let them cool for a bit. While the ornaments were cooling, we helped cover the card table with newspaper as Mom brought out different colors of paint and brushes. The rest of the afternoon was spent carefully coloring each ornament and running string through each of the holes.

Once the ornaments were dry, we set a few aside to give away as gifts and hung the rest on the garland that Dad had hung around the house.

Later that evening, Mom and I went to deliver a few salt dough ornaments as gifts. We first walked to Mimi and Bompa's letting the light from the dusk-to-dawn light lead our way. The smell of wet leaves and smoke from my grandparents' and great-grandparents' fireplaces filled the air. As we took the short walk from our house to theirs, I carefully stepped on some of the leaves to see if I could hear them crunch. It was to no avail, though; all the leaves were too damp and had lost their crunching ability.

We quietly opened the screen and creaked open the white wooden door that led into their living room. The smell of burning wood, onions, and coffee filled the room. Mimi was sitting on the yellow couch in the living room, smoking a cigarette, and reading a book. She was a little hunched over with short gray hair and a big smile.

"Hello," she said, putting down both her cigarette and book to embrace me in a warm hug.

"We made a little something for you." Mom handed her the ornaments.

Mimi's eyes lit up. "Oh, these are so pretty!" She motioned toward the family room. "Go show them to Maynard."

Mom and I walked through the living room, past the long white breakfast bar, through the Dutch door that was split in half, and into the family room. Bompa was sitting tall in his armchair, watching TV. He was of much bigger stature than Mimi and still had some streaks of black hair mixed in with his gray. His big green leather chair sat close to the big shiny brown piano that was covered with framed pictures of the family. I had been told many times the piano was an antique that was, "shipped from overseas around the horn."

"Hi, Bomp," said Mom.

"Well, hello. What brings you two over?"

"We wanted to give you these."

Bompa took the ornaments from Mom's hand and held them up to the light.

"Timmy, did you make these?" He looked right at me. For some reason, until I was an adult, he thought my name was Timmy instead of Kimmy, but I didn't mind the nickname.

Mom motioned to me. "We all did."

"They're beautiful. Go ahead and hang them somewhere on the tree." He pointed toward the beautifully decorated fake green

Christmas tree that stood in the corner of their family room. The bright Christmas lights flashed on and off. He turned to Mom. "How's Clint doing?"

I took the ornaments and put them on the tree as Mom talked for a few minutes to Bompa about how Clint's treatments were going. I was done putting the ornaments on a few limbs, and she wrapped up the conversation.

"We have to go deliver the others to Mom and Dad, but we'll see you again soon." Mom gave him a hug.

After Mom and I said our goodbyes to Mimi and Bompa, we walked over to my grandparents' house.

"Knock, knock," Mom said as we walked into their house. The smell of warmth filled the air.

"We don't want any," Papa said, chuckling to himself.

"But we have ornaments," I said excitedly.

"Oh, let me see." Grandma eagerly stepped away from the card table where she was working on a puzzle. She set a piece down to take the ornaments. She held them carefully, inspecting the paint on each one.

"How's Clint today?" Papa asked

"Here, Kimmy, you help me find a spot for these." Grandma led me over to their beautifully decorated fake bluish-green Christmas tree in the corner of their living room. Grandma and I found spots for each ornament, then we went into the kitchen while Mom and Papa talked about the latest updates on Clint.

Grandma took the lid off the cookie jar that sat on their kitchen table. "Do you want a cookie?"

"What kind are they?"

"Oh, they're just store-bought taffy cookies. They're my favorite, though. Try one."

I reached my hand in and pulled out one that looked like a miniature sandwich. It was two brown rectangles with ridges, which made stripes on them, with white cream in the middle. I took a bite and was surprised by its sweetness.

"Mmm…yum."

"I knew you'd like them."

"Do you know any Christmas carols?" she asked as I climbed onto a barstool.

I tried to remember what a Christmas carol was. "I don't think so."

"Have you heard this one? *You better watch out, You better not cry, Better not pout, I'm telling you why Santa Claus is coming to town…*"

She continued singing the words to the song, "Santa Claus is Coming to Town," as I continued eating my cookie. I loved listening to her sing.

"He sees you when you're sleepin', He knows when you're awake, He knows if you've been bad or good…"

She shook her finger toward me as she sang the last line, *"So be good for goodness sake,"* reminding me to be good or else Santa Claus wouldn't bring me any presents.

Mom walked into the kitchen. "Ready to go home? It's time for Clint to take his medicine, and I need to make sure that your dad hasn't gotten Cody too wound up before bed."

"Yep, I'm ready." I finished the last bite of my cookie.

"I hope you've been better than I've been," Papa hollered out. "That fat ol' devil never brings me anything. Not even coal!"

We all laughed, then Mom and I walked hand in hand back to our house as the fireplace smoke and the smell of wet leaves lingered in the air. Even though Clint was sick and dying, we could still find joy in each moment of life as they came.

The fake fireplace we put up in our house every Christmas.

15

CHRISTMAS EVE

New traditions are made when we
aren't trying to create them.

~KIMBERLEY'S THOUGHT~

THINKING THAT the day couldn't get there soon enough, Christmas Eve morning had finally arrived! Clint and I spent the morning lounging around in our pajamas, too excited to do much of anything else except talk about Christmas. As lunch time approached, Mom reminded us that we'd be going to Bill and Donna Grunloh's house for a potluck to celebrate Christmas Eve day with them, Ben and Mary, and some of our other family friends.

Clint and I quickly changed into good clothes and picked out two of the best salt-dough ornaments that we'd made to take to them as gifts. Mom and Dad gathered the salami, cheese, and crackers that they'd prepared to share at the potluck, picked up Cody and some of his toys, and then hurried us all out to the car.

We took the short drive to Bill and Donna's and parked in front of their house. As soon as we opened their front door, we were greeted with warmth from their fireplace, welcoming hellos, and friendly hugs. The smell of fresh pine from their Christmas tree, recently ground coffee beans, and freshly baked cookies filled the air. Bill's dad, Rudy, sat in their large rocking chair by the fireplace.

We all greeted Rudy; surprised to see him. He didn't live in California, so it was always special when he was there.

He smiled. "Hello!" giving us a little wave. Rudy was the oldest person in the room with a full head of gray hair and eyes that sparkled like magic. He continued rocking in the heavy wooden rocking chair, and I ran over to him and gave him a big hug. He instantly started telling us about his newest adventure, of how he made it driving in the snow from Minnesota to Bill and Donna's house in time for Christmas. We listened intently to every word as he shared each detail. I loved listening to his stories, and the longer I listened, the more he told.

The rest of our friends got everything out for the potluck, and soon it was time to eat.

"Look at this!" Mom pulled me from Rudy to the round wooden dining room table.

"What is it?" I peered over the green, round thing sitting in the middle of the table.

Mom explained, "They were just telling me that it's a cornflake wreath. I just had a little bite of it. It tastes kind of like Rice Crispy Treats, but different. It's made from cornflakes and marshmallows. They added green food coloring to make it look like a wreath and put little red hot candies on it to look like holly berries. Try it."

"Mmm…that's really good!"

"We'll have to try making that one day. Maybe next year," said Mom.

It wasn't until I was in high school that we finally tried making the cornflake wreath for ourselves. It's now a Christmas tradition in our family.

We spent the next few hours snacking, playing with the kids that were there, visiting with our grown-up friends, and exchanging presents. We finally said our goodbyes then headed back to our house for Clint to take his medicine and to get a little rest.

Soon it was time for dinner and another excursion. We all piled back into the car and drove through the light fog to my friend Karla's house, who lived close to us in the country. This was the home of my parents' friends and their daughter who was one of my best friends. As we walked into their house, we were led into their newly added-on step-down living room, where their giant ten foot plus Christmas tree stood. It was the focal point of the entire place, filling the room with all its grandeur. Presents were neatly stacked under it, waiting to be opened as white lights twinkled with all their glory. I was in awe, admiring the beautiful Christmas tree.

Karla pulled on my arm, eager to show me some of her new toys as she led Clint, Cody, and me to her bedroom to play with her and the other kids. The grown-ups sat at the bar and talked while dinner finished cooking. Once it was ready, we ate in kind of a rush because my parents wanted to get back home before the fog settled in too thick. As my dad drove, he joked about how Rudolph might even have trouble finding his way in that thick fog.

I really hoped that he was wrong.

Once we were settled at home, Mom called Grandma, Papa, Mimi, and Bompa over to watch the play that Clint and I had been rehearsing all week. We put on our pajamas and hid in the bedroom, practicing our lines, patiently waiting for everyone to get there. Once our grandparents and great-grandparents had arrived, Clint and I peeked our heads out of our bedroom to see where everyone was sitting. We made our way into the living room and acted like professional actors as Mom narrated the poem, "Willie and Annie's Prayer" by Sophia P. Snow.

Clint and I acted out the parts of Willie and Annie, trying hard to remember our lines. Mom helped guide us along, reminding us of key words as we did our best.

"Good job!" Everyone clapped as we wrapped up the last few lines.

Clint then ran into our bedroom and came out wearing a fake Santa beard. He then busted out with the lyrics of Santa Claus is Coming to Town, "*You better watch out, you better not cry...*" and everyone laughed.

I tried hard to sing with him, but I couldn't remember all the words. I was hoping that Grandma would remind me, but even though it was just family there, she was too embarrassed to sing in front of so many people. She would usually only sing songs with just me when nobody else was around.

After the laughter and singing had died down, Dad put a Christmas album on the record player. We gathered close to the Christmas tree that was fully lit with colorful Christmas lights and listened to Gene Autry singing, "Rudolph the Red-Nosed Reindeer." A pile of presents that Mom had spent hours wrapping several days before sat underneath it. Clint and Dad looked for the presents that had "Christmas Eve" and someone's name on them. They then passed out one Christmas present to each of us.

Mom reminded us, "Remember, we only open one present on Christmas Eve."

"That's right," Grandma agreed.

Papa reinforced with a big smile. "The rest are for you to open tomorrow morning."

We each took our turn opening a present as everyone else smiled and shared excitement in what each person got. I don't remember exactly what each one was, but Christmas Eve presents were usually something small and simple, like a pair of gloves or slippers. After presents were opened, we all said our goodnights to Grandma, Papa, Mimi, and Bompa; as they were leaving, we heard what sounded to me like sleigh bells.

Suddenly the door flew open. "HO, HO, HO!"

We all watched in amazement as someone dressed as Santa Claus walked right in through our sliding glass door.

"HO, HO, HO! MERRY CHRISTMAS!"

"Santa!" we kids shouted.

"I came to say hello before I have to get back and help Santa with delivering the rest of the presents."

It kind of sounded like Dad's voice, but it didn't look anything like him.

Clint looked right at the man. "Is that you, Dad?"

"It's one of Santa's helpers," said Mom. "Your dad is in the bathroom." She hollered out, "Hurry up, Gene, one of Santa's helpers is here!"

Clint whispered to me, "It looks just like Dad, though. Look at his eyes."

Mom must have heard him. "A lot of people's eyes look the same."

"I really need to get going. I just came to give you these." Santa handed each of us a candy cane. "Do you have anything to clean my boots. I think I stepped in reindeer poop." He pretended to clean his boots off on our carpet.

"Ewe!" We all laughed.

"Okay, let me get a picture of all of you with Santa's helper before he has to leave. Shoot, I sure wish your Dad could see this." Mom gathered us up to sit on the helper's lap.

Mom snapped a few pictures, and just as quickly as he came, Santa's helper was gone.

Grandma, Papa, Mimi, and Bompa announced that they needed to get home before Santa came with our presents, and they walked out the door.

I ran to my bedroom window to watch them as they walked to their houses, but they disappeared into the thick white sea of fog as soon as they made it to the Quonset. I wondered if Rudolph could help Santa find his way to our house in fog so thick.

My thoughts were quickly jolted as I heard Dad's voice in the family room.

"Who was here?"

"It was Santa!" I sprinted to him from my bedroom.

"No, it was one of Santa's helpers." Clint corrected me.

"It was? I can't believe I missed him."

I was really sad for my dad for a second before Mom interrupted. "Go get our pajamas on, we need to hurry and read, *The Night Before Christmas*, it's a tradition!"

I ran out of my bedroom carrying my big doll. By the time I got there, Mom was sitting in the gold chair holding Cody in her lap, along with the Little Golden Book of *The Night Before Christmas*.

Clint was sitting at her feet, and as soon as I sat on the floor next to him, Mom started to read, "Twas the night before Christmas and all through the house…"

When she finished the last words, our eyes were heavy.

Mom read softly, "…and to all a good night."

Dad walked in from the kitchen. "We can't forget the milk and cookies for Santa."

Clint jumped up. "That's right!"

We went into the kitchen to help Dad get a few Lemon Cooler cookies, my favorite, and put them on a plate. He poured a glass of milk, and we set both on the breakfast bar where Santa was sure to see them.

Clint and I headed off to bed. Mom and Dad put Cody in his crib while I climbed up onto Clint's bed to sleep with him for the night. There was no way I was going to be able to fall asleep in my own bed on Christmas Eve!

Mom and Dad came in to tuck us in.

"Remember, don't go sneaking into the living room too early in the morning," Mom reminded us. "We want to be there when you see what Santa brought you."

"We won't," I promised.

"I'll make sure Kim doesn't sneak in there without me." Clint pretended to hold me hostage on his bed.

Mom and Dad each kissed their index finger, reached up to Clint's bed, and touched our foreheads.

"Let visions of sugar plums dance in your head." Mom smiled.

"What are sugar plums?" I wondered out loud.

Mom added, "Plums that are covered in sugar."

"Yuck!" I scowled.

Dad laughed. "Think of counting reindeer instead. Get some sleep."

Mom and Dad left our room, and we agreed not to get up too early. Clint and I lay in his bed trying to spot Santa's sleigh out the window through the heavy fog. It seemed like hours, but sure enough, we finally drifted off to sleep.

Santa or one of his helpers coming to see us at our house Christmas Eve 1983. Clint, Cody, Santa, and me.

SANTA IS COMING

~KIMBERLEY'S THOUGHT~

I WAS SUDDENLY AWAKENED by a clanking sound. "What's that?"

"Maybe it's Santa up on the roof," Clint answered sleepily.

"No, I think we've been asleep too long for it to be Santa. I think he's already been here. But it is still dark outside." I lay there as stiff as a board.

What if it was Santa?

Clint and I lay motionless for several minutes, waiting to hear another sound. Maybe the sound of Santa's sleigh bells is what we were listening for. Then we heard what sounded like dishes clanking in the kitchen.

"It must be Mom and Dad," we both said at almost the exact same time.

Mom and Dad must be up.

Suddenly I realized that we could get up and open presents.

"Christmas is here!" I scrambled down the ladder from Clint's bed.

He quickly followed behind me, and we both hurried into Cody's room.

He was still sound asleep.

"Merry Christmas," Clint whispered to Cody.

"It's time to get up and open presents," I said in my high-pitched voice, hoping that the news would excite Cody enough to wake up.

Finally, Dad came into Cody's room, lifted him out of his crib, and carried him into the living room. Clint and I followed and joined Mom in the living room.

It was still dark outside; the Christmas tree was the only light inside the house, creating an ambiance of peace and calm. Even in the dimly lit room, we could quickly see that Santa had been there and left large presents for Clint, Cody, and me.

"It looks like Santa has been here." Dad laid Cody on a blanket by the Christmas tree and near what appeared to be a giant white plastic tunnel of sorts. Cody curled up into a ball and started to drift back to sleep.

 Clint and I ran over to the colorfully lit tree to see what Santa had left us.

I couldn't believe my eyes; there was a little red stroller with my big doll sitting inside it. A little red stroller just for me! Santa must have known how heavy my big doll could be when I carried her everywhere. I picked up my big doll and held her tight.

Clint looked at the new black BMX bike that Santa had left him, and we both gushed with excitement over what Santa had brought Cody. At the entrance to the white plastic tunnel was a blue and white Smurf train engine big enough for Cody to sit on. The little riding toy had a yellow handle on the back so we could push it around. Cody's eyes lit up when the little balls on the front of the engine popped when Clint pushed it around the living room.

"And what is this thing?" Clint lifted a white plastic cave-looking thing that curved around toward the back of the Christmas tree.

"I think it's a tunnel." Mom pulled it away from the tree and stretched it across the living room. "Santa must have left it for all three of you kids."

"What do we do with it?" I asked.

"You crawl through it, like this." Mom demonstrated by getting down on all fours and crawled from one end of the tunnel to the other.

I clapped my hands together. "How fun!"

Clint and I raced through the tunnel, crawling as quickly as we could. Cody finally woke up enough to join us, crawling through quicker than any of us.

After several minutes of playing with the tunnel and moving it around in different shapes, Mom helped me put my big doll back in her new stroller. Dad went into the family room to put a *Statler Brothers Christmas* album on the record player. It added a peaceful sound through the speakers that were placed near the ceiling throughout the house.

We gathered at the red and white fake fireplace to see what Santa had left in our stockings.

We sat down on the carpet and watched Clint as he pulled things one by one out of his stocking. Santa had left him a book of Lifesavers, a large plastic candy cane filled with M&M's, a few Hot Wheels Cars, and more candy. He then helped Cody look through his stocking to see what treasures he had inside. One by one, we looked through our stockings to see what goodies Santa had left us. I, too, had a book of Lifesavers, a large plastic candy cane filled with M&M's, and more candy. Each of us also had a few other things that Santa had given us that he knew we would like. I was amazed that Santa knew each of us so well.

Once the stockings had been thoroughly looked through, Dad hollered, "Time to open presents!" He was acting more like the kid in the family than an adult.

We each found a comfortable spot to sit on the floor as Dad changed the record to a different album. Once he returned to the living room, Dad sat close to the Christmas tree and looked at the names on the neatly wrapped presents. He gave a present to Clint first. We all watched Clint open it to see what he got, then Dad found a present with my name on it. Next, it was Cody's turn, followed by Mom, and then Dad. We each took turns opening presents, watching with anticipation to see what each family member received. The mountain of presents under the tree slowly dwindled to our "Open Me Last" present as the living room brightened with the sun rising to officially start Christmas Day.

It wasn't until years later that I learned how my parents had to borrow money from friends that Christmas in hopes of giving us kids the best Christmas ever. Money was very tight because of rising medical bills, but knowing that it very well might have been Clint's last Christmas, they wanted to make it the best possible for all of us. Christmas that year didn't really feel any different to me than any other, though, as each one always felt like the best Christmas ever.

After all the presents were opened, we had a huge pile of wrapping paper, boxes, and bows in the middle of the living room floor. It mimicked a huge pile of fallen leaves that had just been raked up. Clint, Cody, and I were busy looking through all the presents that we had recently opened when Mom left the room to put cinnamon rolls in the oven for breakfast.

Dad stood and walked to the other side of the living room. We assumed that he was heading into the kitchen to help Mom with breakfast, but he had other plans.

"Cannonball!" he yelled and got a running start before jumping into the heap of wrapping paper mess.

We all broke into laughter at Dad's silliness.

"Who's next?"

We each took turns jumping into the pile.

We spent the next little while rebuilding the pile, jumping in it, covering each other up with wrapping paper, and trying to hide. After having fun in the wrapping paper mess, Dad left the room to get a large garbage sack. When he returned, we all helped stuff the torn and shredded wrapping paper into the black garbage sack.

The smell of cinnamon rolls and eggs cooking filled the air.

"Save the bows!" Mom called from the kitchen.

"Oh, that's right. Help me save the bows," Dad said in a hushed voice as he looked through the garbage sack for any bows that he might have mistakenly thrown away.

We quickly pulled all the bows out of the pile before stuffing the rest of the paper into the sack. It was a family tradition that Grandma Pierce had started many years before to save money. She'd save the bows from the Christmas presents each year and reuse them for years and years to come. We carried on with the tradition with our own family, always having a box full of bows in the closet for all occasions.

We spent the next few hours playing with our new toys and eating a scrumptious Christmas breakfast of cinnamon rolls, eggs, sausage, strawberries, and milk. After we'd cleaned up the breakfast dishes, we all got dressed in our good clothes; Levi's and sweatshirts.

Mom and Dad gathered the last few remaining presents that had been set aside for other members of the family. We walked past the Quonset hut to my grandparents' house to celebrate Christmas with the rest of the extended family.

"Knock, knock, Merry Christmas!" Mom opened the door, and we walked into the house she was raised in.

"Merry Christmas!" called Grandma and Papa.

Mom and Dad set the presents under their tree while Clint and Papa went outside to get more firewood. After just a few minutes, they both came in carrying an armful of logs.

"Who wants to see colors on the fire?" Papa set his armful of wood in the large brass log holder.

"ME!" Clint, Cody, and I shouted at the same time.

"Okay, everyone, come over here to the fire."

Papa pulled back the black mesh wire screen at the front of the fireplace, grabbed a log out of Clint's arms, placed it on the already burning fire, and sparks flew.

Cody and I sat on the gray and white marble hearth in front of the fireplace. Clint picked up a cylinder-shaped canister that said "Seymor Color Flame Crystals" on the front. He handed it to Papa. "Here you go."

"Are you ready to see colors?" Papa asked again.

We all stared at the fire as Papa sprinkled powder from the canister onto the burning logs. Instantly, the flames went from the normal red, orange, and yellow, to blue, green, and purple.

"So pretty!" I couldn't take my eyes off the colorful flames.

"Oooo…" Cody watched intently.

"That's cool!" added Clint.

"Knock, Knock, Merry Christmas!" came shouts from the back door off the kitchen.

My cousins, aunts, and uncles slowly started to arrive. Everyone was carrying presents; they set their food on the kitchen table or placed in the refrigerator, where it would remain until it was time for Christmas dinner.

The presents were all set near and under the Christmas tree in the corner of the living room. After hellos, we each found our spots to sit and open them.

There were no actual assigned spots for us on Christmas morning, but each of us had what we called our *special spots* where we traditionally sat for this fun tradition. My cousin Kerry and I sat on the green and gold living room carpet between the TV and Grandma's and Papa's chairs. Mom and Dad sat on the couch against the wall on the south side of the living room. My aunts, uncles, and other cousins sat near the fireplace, on the marble seat, on the floor, and in chairs that had been brought in from the kitchen. Papa sat in his big leather reclining chair, and somehow, Clint managed to snag Grandma's large reclining chair that sat right next to Papa's. Since Clint was in Grandma's chair, she carried a chair in from the kitchen table and sat in it at the edge of the living room, which gave her quick access to the bathroom and kitchen if needed while we were all opening presents.

Papa crouched down in front of the Christmas tree. "Who wants to open presents?"

"ME!" everyone shouted.

"Wait, wait, I have to go to the bathroom first."

"GRAAANNNDDDMAAAAA!" we all hollered.

"I'll be quick." She disappeared into the kitchen.

"Well, I guess we wait," Papa said, and we all laughed.

"Okay, I'm back." Grandma made a grand entrance back into the living room.

"Good, who wants to open presents now?" Papa asked again.

"ME!" we all shouted a second time.

Papa gave his best chuckle. "Well then, let's get this show on the road. Clint, do you want to be my helper? I'll be Santa, and you can be one of my elves."

"Sure!" Clint jumped up from the spot that he'd claimed in Grandma's big chair.

Papa read the name on each present out loud and handed them to Clint who took the gifts to each person. All of us were overly excited, and we waited patiently until the last name was read on the last package. Then we waited for the signal to start unwrapping.

"Okay, that's the last one. What are you all waiting for, open your presents!" Papa grinned from ear to ear as he walked back to his chair.

We all began opening our treasures while gushing with excitement over what everyone else got. My cousin Kerry and I had to time it just right to open our presents at the exact same time because Grandma always bought us exactly the same thing.

"Thank you, thank you, thank you…" could be heard around the living room as each gift was revealed.

"Wait, there's more!" Bompa said as he walked into the living room holding a stack of white envelopes.

He called off our names one by one, and we each took turns walking over to him to get our envelope. Finally, it was my turn.

"Timmy," he said, and everyone quietly chuckled.

Once all the envelopes were given out, he said, "Well, open them up."

We quickly opened our envelopes, and we all squealed with excitement, seeing the green bill that was nicely nested inside. I don't remember the exact amount that we all got, but it was ours, and that's all that mattered. We each tucked our money away in secret spots and expressed our thanks.

"Thank you, Bompa!" we all squealed more than once.

"You're welcome. Merry Christmas!" and he walked out the back door.

After he left and after all the presents were opened, Papa brought in a big black garbage sack for us to throw our colorful, used wrapping paper into.

"Save the bows!" Grandma hollered.

We all laughed, wondering how old the bows were by now.

"Might as well save the boxes, too," said Papa.

"And the paper!" added Grandma.

"No, no, no, throw the paper away." Papa wadded a bunch and threw it in the garbage sack.

We all helped each other to sort out what needed to be saved from what we would throw away and cleaned up the living room. We spent some time visiting as my uncles carted their family's presents to their cars. We gathered our gifts and carried them back to our house.

Once we were home, Clint took his medicine and a nap while the rest of us relaxed. We ate some lunch, looked through our new presents, baked, cooked, and watched Christmas cartoons on TV. We spent the afternoon just enjoying being a family.

Mom and I baked and decorated two eight-inch round cakes with Santa Claus's face on them while Mom also made a side dish of scalloped potatoes to contribute to the dinner that we'd soon be eating at Grandma and Papa's house. At about 4:00 p.m., we went back to my grandparents' house.

"Mmmm… It smells like the ham is almost ready," Mom announced as we walked into Grandma and Papa's house.

"It sure is," said Papa. The sweet smell of freshly baked ham filled the air.

"Let's put all the food over there," said Grandma. She motioned toward the table covered with a plastic green and red Christmas cloth.

The table was loaded with various fruit and vegetable dishes, potatoes, rolls, Grandma's homemade coleslaw, carrot cake, and so much more.

"This all looks good enough to eat," said Dad.

"I hope so, that's what it's there for." Papa chuckled.

Mom added the Santa Claus cakes and scalloped potatoes to the mix. Christmas dinner was going to be amazing!

"I've got the fruitcake!" said Grandma.

"Uggh…" We all groaned.

"My mom sent it to us," explained Grandma. "She made it with gumdrops instead of real fruit this year. You might really like it."

I think Grandma was in hopes we would all try it. But we all made faces of disgust.

"Ham's done!" Papa set it on the bar. "Who wants to watch me slice it?"

We all squished into the tiny kitchen, the best that we could, to watch Papa slice the ham. The pieces fell one by one onto the giant platter with juices gently cascading down the sides of them.

My stomach growled at the sight of it.

Once it was fully sliced, Papa said, "Time to dish up!"

We formed a line at the front of the kitchen table, each took a large paper plate and filled them with as much food as they would hold. One by one, we made our way into the living room to find a spot to sit and eat. Kerry and I claimed our spots on the floor in front of the TV where the football game was blaring.

The fire burning in the fireplace kept the house cozy and warm. We spent the evening eating, talking, playing games, and watching the football game. We all took that evening for granted, thinking that we'd all be together for Christmas every year.

Christmas traditions that we assumed would carry on through the ages. It was a day that I wish I could have back. A day that I wish I could have frozen in time. The one thing that can be guaranteed in life, though, is that nothing ever stays the same.

Christmas morning 1983.
The year that Santa brought a red stroller for my big doll.

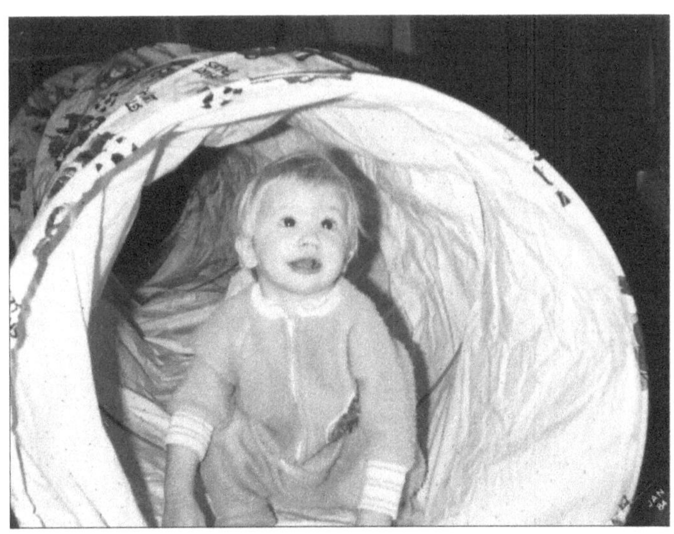

Cody exploring the tunnel that Santa brought
all of us for Christmas 1983.

HAPPY NEW YEAR

The start of each new year is a reminder
that there is hope for the future.

"HAPPY NEW YEAR!" Bill and Donna announced their entrance into our house in celebration. Mom and Dad were in the kitchen preparing food, and country music played on the radio.

I ran to them blowing a green cardboard party horn as loud as I could. "Happy New Year!"

"Oh, come on, you can blow it louder than that, can't you?" Donna laughed and made her way past our pool table.

"Try again," Bill encouraged me to blow my little horn louder.

Encouraged by their prompting, I tried to give my cardboard horn a rhythmic toot, toot.

We were celebrating New Year's Eve at our house, with my grandparents, a few cousins, my parents' friends, and their kids. Bill and Donna were the first to arrive, and the other guests soon followed. I stood guard close to our sliding glass door, welcoming each guest as they arrived.

Clint and Cody appeared to greet Diane Dallas and her two

boys tooting their own cardboard horns. The celebration for ringing in the new year was about to begin.

After it seemed as if most of the guests had arrived, I walked over to the breakfast bar to see what scrumptious treats were already out to eat. Mary, who was about the same age as my parents, was just uncovering her bowl of famous potato salad and setting it among the sea of other side dishes.

"Do you want a bite?" Mary asked me.

"Yes!" I already knew it was going to be delicious because I'd eaten her famous potato salad many times before.

She put some on a plate for me, and we chatted for a bit as I took a few bites. Soon, other familiar faces gathered around the breakfast bar to make plates of food for themselves. The kitchen became crowded, so I ran off to find my friends who were playing in other parts of the house.

"Do you want to play hide-and-go-seek?" Clint asked when he saw me.

"Sure!" I tried to sound like it was the best idea ever. New Year's Eve and New Year's Day were the hardest days of the year for my big brother because it was on New Year's Day that he was first diagnosed with leukemia. A memory that always haunted him, and New Year's Eve was the trigger to that dreadful memory. He spent many New Year's Eves becoming a recluse to most around him, so his wanting to play something on that evening was a welcome sight.

Clint and I went through the house to find all the kids who wanted to join us in the game. We played several rounds of hide-and-go-seek for a while, then became distracted by everything else that was going on. The adults were spread throughout the house talking, *Dick Clark's New Years Rockin' Eve* was blaring on the television in the living room. My dad and his friends were playing their guitars, forming their own little band, in the family room, and we were all keeping an eye on the clock to ensure that we didn't miss the countdown to the new year.

All of us kids gathered in the kitchen to grab snacks. Then Clint made his way back to our bedroom to play with his train with most of the other kids following behind him. I wandered into the family room and stood by the pool table, wishing that I were big enough to play the game.

"I'm too worried that you'll scratch the table because you aren't quite tall enough to hold the pool cue at the right height yet." My mom's words played in my head.

"Let's just play with the pool balls," said one of my friends who I didn't even realize was standing beside me.

"Okay." My eyes lit up in agreement. I thought it was a good idea.

We reached down to the rectangular opening where most of the balls were sitting and placed them on the green felt cover. Then, we went around the table, reaching down into the pockets and pulling out all the remaining balls. We lined them up at the far end of the table and started blasting them toward the holes with as much force as we could in hopes they would land in one of the pockets. The more quickly we rolled them, the more excited we got about being the first one to sink a ball. We had no realization that our fingers could have been crushed in the process, with balls ricocheting everywhere. The quicker we moved, the louder the balls clanked against one another, which caught my mom's attention.

She walked over to the pool table to take a closer look at what we were doing. "Okay, time to play that game a different way." Mom used her serious mom voice.

My friend and I looked at each other with sheepish grins, knowing that we'd been caught doing something we probably shouldn't have been doing but still not realizing we could have been hurt.

We gathered all the balls against the far end of the pool table and took turns rolling them for a while until we were interrupted by Donna setting a box on the table.

"What's that?" I asked.

"It's all the goodies for us to use to count down to the New Year. Do you guys want to help me spread them out?"

"Sure!" we said together.

The box was full of different colored beads, horns, streamers, confetti, noisemakers, hats, and tiaras. Everyone gathered around to help spread out all the contents of the box.

"Pick something to use to help with the countdown," Mom said to everyone within earshot.

I picked out a blue noisemaker that made a loud clanking noise when you spun it around by its white handle and a paper party horn that unrolled when I blew into it. Too excited to see what everyone else picked out, I ran into the living room and looked at the TV. From the countdown clock I could see that we only had five minutes left before the new year began.

Dick Clark was on TV at Times Square in New York City, talking about something, but I was too focused on the big ball all lit up with red and green lights. It looked more like an apple than a ball. I knew that right at midnight it would drop, and we would all ring in the new year with lots of noise and cheer. All us kids gathered close in front of the TV and watched the seconds on the clock tick away.

Clint wasn't standing next to me; instead, he was sitting in one of the gold chairs near the wall toward the back of the living room. He was exhausted from a very busy evening, and maybe a bit depressed.

Finally, it was time to start counting down. "..., five, four, three, two, one – HAPPY NEW YEAR!!!"

Everyone shouted as the big red apple dropped in Times Square, and the number 1984 lit up in white lights at the bottom of the screen. Surrounded by family and close friends, we rang in the new year together.

Standing in back, Grandma Pierce and Papa
Front, Great Grandparents Bompa and Mimi

DYING

Just because life comes to an end, doesn't mean that it didn't happen and that it wasn't amazing.

~KIMBERLEY'S THOUGHT~

THE NEW YEAR had begun, and winter rapidly turned into spring. The changing of the seasons, however, didn't change how Clint, at ten years old, was still fighting his battle against both leukemia and testicular cancer. In early spring, he had to be hospitalized. My parents, once again, took turns staying with him for days on end while the other one managed all the affairs at home, including taking care of Cody and me.

On days when both of my parents needed to be with Clint at the hospital, and I needed to go to school, I stayed with family or friends. It was a cycle that continually repeated itself for several months. One weekend, I was able to spend some time with my whole family at Oakland Children's Hospital.

I walked into Clint's tiny hospital room. "Hi! Where's the window seat?"

"This room doesn't have one." Clint clicked through the channels. His priority was always that his hospital room had a well-working television set hanging on the wall. My one request was that it had a window seat to the outside world. A request that was a little harder to make a reality than the TV was.

I scooted onto Clint's bed with him for a while and watched TV while Mom, Dad, and Cody went for a walk. Clint and I were in good hands with his room being close to the nurses' station. They constantly checked on us. Clint really wasn't feeling well, though, so it didn't take long before he was sound asleep, and I was stuck watching something boring on TV until Mom and Dad returned.

"Hey, Pumpkin," Dad whispered. "Do you want to go for a walk with me?"

"Yes. Is Freida here?" I asked.

"Let's go find out."

Clint's room was a tight squeeze for all of us to be in at one time, so Dad, Cody, and I spent the next little while visiting with Freida and wandering the hospital hallways while Mom stayed with Clint. After we had our fill of visiting the nurses, doctors, hospital staff, and other families, we wandered back to Clint's room. He looked a little better after getting some rest and was eager to get out of bed.

"Do you want to go for a walk?" Dad asked him.

"Yeah, I want to go and see my friends."

"Okay, let's do it then." Dad helped Clint get out of bed. Mom secured Clint's hospital gown and stabilized the cords on the IV pole to prepare it for transport, something that she and my dad had done hundreds of times before.

While they were busy doing that, Cody and I played with Coco, Clint's puppet, and my big doll. Cody and I prepared Coco for transport, too, by attaching him to Clint's IV pole with Coco's Velcro hands.

"Coco fits well on my IV pole," said Clint. "I wonder how my friends are doing?" He'd become friends with many patients over the years, and he always hoped that they would get better. Some had beaten the odds and were now out of the hospital for good. That always lifted his spirits and added to his hope.

Mom and Cody settled into Clint's room while Dad and I prepared to help Clint visit with his friends. Dad helped him walk to the nurses' station in the hall of the fourth floor while I walked closely next to him and his IV pole. With my big doll in my arms, I kept a close eye on Coco to make sure he didn't fall off. We stopped at the nurse's station to check and see if anyone we knew was currently staying in nearby rooms.

We recognized the names of a few of the patients, so we went to their rooms to say, "hi." The visits were short, and I stayed in the hallway for most of them so as not to crowd the small rooms. Having more than one IV pole in a room was sometimes cumbersome, in addition to the grown-ups.

Lastly, we made our way to Minnie's room. Minnie had been in the hospital for quite some time, so we knew exactly where his room was. Minnie was someone with whom Clint had gotten to be good friends, and our families had become close as well. Minnie and Clint had spent a lot of time in the hospital together. Minnie was a boy who had been battling ALL, the same type of leukemia that Clint had.

We went into Minnie's room expecting to see his smiling face, but we quickly discovered that he was no longer there, and there wasn't any sign of his family anywhere either. Dad went to the nurse's desk to ask where Minnie and his family were, hoping that they had been moved to a different room or, better yet, hoping that they had been discharged from the hospital.

The nurses sadly told us the news of Minnie's passing, and we were all in shock. My dad did his best to compose himself as Clint started to cry. The grief struck him hard, hearing the unexpected news, and his tears soon turned into anger as we numbly made our way back to his hospital room. I didn't know what to think or how to feel. Even though I had been told about death my whole life, I still hadn't fully understood what it meant to die. Where exactly was Minnie?

I don't remember much about what happened in the next few hours, I just remember that it was a solemn time as our whole family squeezed into Clint's hospital room. We were all trying to come to grips with the reality of what was happening all around us. It wasn't just our family that was fighting a battle; our friends were all fighting, too, battles that none of us could fully prepare for. The roller coaster of emotions came in waves as we carried on with what each new hour had in store for all of us in that giant children's hospital.

The doctors and nurses at Oakland Children's Hospital were beacons of light on some of the darkest days, and that moment in time was no exception. They, too, were suffering with their own roller coaster of emotions as they said their final goodbyes to some of their patients and helped to keep hope alive for their other ones.

As we were all still processing the loss of Minnie, a nurse walked into Clint's room holding a large bouquet of colorful balloons with white curly ribbon attached to each of them. My heart was instantly lifted upon seeing them. Balloons were pretty, fun, and full of life, yet everyone else still seemed so sad. I couldn't quite understand how anyone could still be sad when there were such pretty balloons in the room.

"Mom, what are the balloons for?" I asked.

"They're for Minnie."

But Minnie wasn't in the hospital. How was he going to get the balloons? My young brain couldn't quite grasp what was happening, so I stood quietly just watching, trying to figure it all out.

Another nurse came into the room with a wheelchair, and before I knew exactly what was going on, the nurse prepared Clinton's IV for travel and helped him get into a wheelchair. The other nurse stood close to the door, still holding onto the beautiful bouquet of balloons that embraced every color of the rainbow.

Slowly, the nurses and Clint made their way into the hallway. Dad carried Cody, and Mom nudged me along into the hallway as well. We were greeted by a few other nurses and two other kids in wheelchairs, with their families. As a group, we went down the elevator and outside. I was amazed to discover that this time we weren't just walking inside of the hospital, but we were actually going outside, *outside*. We journeyed in a small pack together out the hospital doors, into the February afternoon sunshine, and onto the small black-top paved parking lot where our car was parked.

I wasn't sure what was happening, but I knew we weren't leaving the hospital because there was no way Clint's IV pole was going to fit in our car. We all stood in a small group in the center of the parking lot, and the nurse handed each of us a colorful balloon. Some words were spoken, but I can't remember exactly all that was said.

I stood there, tightly holding onto the white ribbon that was tied to my red balloon, watching it gently sway in the sunlight. I looked around at the balloons that everyone else was holding. I wondered if we were going to have a party or maybe play a game with the balloons. It really was a beautiful sight.

"These balloons are going to fly up to Heaven and welcome Minnie there." This was starting to make sense to me now. Minnie had died, so he was in Heaven. We would be letting go of our balloons.

Even though it was a beautiful sunny day, the air suddenly felt dark and heavy. The colorful balloons were no longer fun and pretty. They were filled with sadness because we were going to be giving the balloons to someone that we could no longer see. We would be giving them to Clint's friend, Minnie. Our friend

Minnie. I then quickly realized that I wouldn't get to keep any of the balloons, so that made me sad, too.

Would Minnie be able to see the balloons when they reached him in Heaven? Would the balloons make him happy, or would he be sad, too?

As these thoughts raced through my head, one by one, each person spoke, saying something that they loved about Minnie. I said something, too, but the words escape now. Minnie was a nice boy with a big smile. I just remember that it was hard to think of what to say in that group of people who were all staring at me as I stood there holding my red balloon.

Then, with the direction of one of the nurses, on the count of three, we all let go of our balloons. I held on to mine for a second longer than everyone else in a desperate attempt to keep it forever, then finally let the string slip from my fingers. Everyone was crying as the balloons flew straight up into the blue sky, and they slowly disappeared from our view.

"Those will make him happy," Clint said with tears in his eyes.

The nurses hugged Clint in agreement, then we all slowly made our way back into the hospital, then dispersed in different directions. Not being able to keep my thoughts locked up inside for a moment longer, I blurted out, "Does everyone get balloons when they die?" I asked anyone within earshot who would answer me.

"Not everyone," my mom quietly said matter-of-factly. She held me close to her side.

Clint was released from the hospital the next day, but the days that followed were filled with sadness as everyone continued to grieve the loss of Clint's closest hospital friend. Even my grandparents were saddened by the news. In grieving the loss of Minnie, fear also set in. Clint was expected to die, too, and we all had to prepare ourselves for that reality. The talk of death was commonplace in our household, but it all felt much more real now.

Even though I was only five years old, I lived on a ranch where animals dying were a common occurrence, so death wasn't a totally new concept. I had seen one of our dogs die, cats, lizards, birds, and even my mom's goldfish, but I had never seen a person die. A person dying felt different. When our animals on the ranch died, we dug a hole and buried them under the plum tree that stood tall next to our mailbox.

When Clint died, would we bury him under the plum tree, too? Would we give him balloons in Heaven like we did Minnie? I had so many questions but didn't know how to ask them without making anyone sad.

There was a lot of quiet tension in the house, and one night, my brother and I got into a fight over something silly during dinner. I was probably mad because he took the last piece of garlic bread, or something dumb like that. Siblings often quarrel about dumb stuff. My mom asked us to stop fighting, but we were kids and just couldn't stop ourselves.

"Knock it off, you two," Dad snapped

"But she, but he, but she, but he…" my brother and I went back and forth progressively getting louder as we pointed fingers at each other.

"That's ENOUGH!" Mom shouted as she put her hands over her face. She shook her head slightly and started sobbing.

Clint and I both instantly stopped speaking and stared at Mom. She *never* cried! What was happening?

She quickly composed herself and said, "Don't you guys understand? This might be the last time we all eat dinner together. This might be the last fight that you ever have with each other."

Good.

I hated fighting anyway.

Maybe Clint wouldn't get so mad at me next time for something silly. Maybe I'd be able to eat all the garlic bread next time!

My mom turned and looked right at me. "Kimberley, your brother is dying. He might die." Her voice quivered a little as she quietly spoke the next words, "Please, just don't fight with each other. At least no more fighting tonight. Okay?"

Oh, that's why she was crying. I forgot that my big brother was dying. I forgot that he might die. I forgot that we never knew what day might be his last here with all of us. I was filled with so many emotions all at once. Sadness thinking about how he might die. Mad at myself for not remembering that. Confusion as to when that would happen, or if it would happen. Fear of what death was like. So many emotions. So many questions.

It didn't help matters that my mom and dad had been to visit Clint's teacher at school earlier that day. The visit with his teacher is a conversation that has been repeated in our family many times. It's a reminder of how important it is to think before we speak. Clint had missed a lot of school because of his illness, so they had made arrangements with his teacher and the school to put him on independent study. They went to the school to gather everything they would need to help Clint catch up on his schoolwork.

As the teacher was covering all the material with my parents, she asked the question, "Why am I wasting my time putting all of this together for you if Clint is just going to die anyway?"

Mom didn't blink an eye as her fist swiftly moved across the table, aimed right at the teacher's face. Knowing what my mom's reaction would be, Dad quickly grabbed her arm just in the nick of time before Mom's fist connected with the spot that it was aimed to hit. Mom and Dad both stood right then and there and walked to the principal's office, where a new teacher was assigned to oversee Clint's independent study for the remainder of the school year.

My parents were still processing that incident while Clint and I were bickering about nonsense. Both Mom and Dad had taught us to live for *today* and to not focus too much on what tomorrow would bring, but it had certainly been a rough few weeks.

We ate the rest of our supper in silence as we became lost in our own thoughts about what was happening in our reality. After dinner was over, we helped each other clean up with a little more compassion than usual. Clint then wandered off into his bedroom to play with his train. My dad took his guitar and sat outside on the porch to enjoy what little daylight was left in the evening. My mom sat with Cody in her gold rocking chair, steadily rocking back and forth as he fell asleep in her arms.

I slowly wandered outside to sit on the front porch with my dad. I sat close to him on the wooden steps as I listened to the soft tune of a slow country song dissipating into the evening breeze from his guitar. I quietly listened for a few minutes, staring at the sunset before he asked me, "What's wrong, Pumpkin? You're so quiet."

Little tears started to form in my eyes. "How do I not be scared of dying? How do I not be scared of Clint dying? Are you scared?" The words came tumbling out.

He set down his guitar and held me close to him.

"Everyone handles those thoughts in their own way, so you will have to decide what helps you." He paused, letting me absorb his words.

"When I get sad or scared about death, I just look all around me." He pointed to an area in the yard and said, "See those beautiful flowers over there? See the beautiful trees?" Then he pointed to the sky. "Do you see the big, beautiful sky?" He looked toward the almond orchard across the street from our house. "Do you see the beautiful white blossoms on the almond trees?"

Next, he pointed to the ground and said, "See how green the grass is?" Then, motioning to everything all around us in our yard, he stated, "All of those things help me to not be worried about dying. The beauty that God, or a higher power than us, created all around us makes me so happy. The people and animals that surround me every day, like you kids, your mom, our dogs, all of you, make me so happy! So, that's what I focus on. When I start to get scared or sad, I just forget about those sad feelings and just focus on all the beautiful and happy things, and they help me not to be so sad or scared. Does that make sense?"

My lip started to quiver as a tear rolled down my cheek. "Yeah, that makes some sense. The flowers *are* really pretty."

"Not as pretty as you." He smiled as he picked up his guitar and started strumming.

I ran back into the house feeling a little lighter after learning that my dad was able to be happy about something even when he was sad and scared at the same time. I know now that he wasn't necessarily happy, but he was able to still find joy in all the sadness. I have carried that conversation with me my entire life, and it has helped me more times than I can count.

It is the littlest moments in life that can change our entire being.

SPRING

*The darkness of winter helps us
to fully embrace the light of spring.*

~KIMBERLEY'S THOUGHT~

THE SUN WAS SHINING brightly as the crack of the baseball bat reverberated through the air around us. The ball flew high into the air and landed right into Clint's mitt.

"Good catch!" Dad picked up the bat and handed it to me. "Your turn to hit."

He stood next to me, showing me exactly how to bend my knees and hold the bat.

"Keep your eye on the ball."

A pitcher for the Oakland A's pitched the ball slowly to me.

Crack!

The ball slowly trickled to the second baseman's feet.

I ran to first base as if a firestorm was chasing me.

Our family friends, Bill Grunloh, Dave Irwin, and a few other people in the community had organized a fundraiser with the Oakland A's franchise to help raise money to pay for Clint's insurmountable medical bills. Several Oakland A's baseball players arrived in a large white van in our little town to put on a three-day clinic for all the children who were interested in learning more about the sport.

Livingston was a town that came together in times of crisis, and baseball was life for many people in the community, so combining baseball with a family in need of help made the turnout all that much more.

In order to lift Clint's spirits, a van load of baseball players arrived at our house early one evening. They said they wanted to encourage our family to keep fighting for Clint's survival. I don't remember the players or managers by name, but I remember their smiles and their kind hearts. Along with other gifts, they brought shiny green and yellow Oakland A's jackets for each of us. After we'd tried them on, one of the players handed me a stuffed bear that was wearing an Oakland A's hat and jersey. That little bear became one of my most prized possessions. I'm sure the players brought gifts for Clint and Cody as well, but I was too focused on my little bear, so I have no idea what presents were given to them, and I never thought to ask.

Mom had cooked dinner for all the players, so we were able to visit with each of them. There wasn't room for all of them to sit at our breakfast bar, so they spread out into the family and living rooms. Some stood and held their plates while they talked amongst themselves. My brothers, Mom, Dad, and I were too excited with their presence to eat a bite of food, but we made sure they were entertained by our conversation.

After dinner, the players went to a hotel. The next few days were filled with baseball fun. My mom prepared breakfast and lunch for them each day to ensure that they were well fed. Blueberry Hill Café, the local diner in town, fed them dinner the last day as a thank you for their arrival in our community. The presence of the baseball players not only lifted the spirits of our family, but they also brought encouragement to the whole town. It seemed the renewal of hope could be felt in the hearts of many.

One of the baseball players told a group of kids, "You all did such a good job today! We hope to see you soon at one of our games." He handed a stack of game tickets to my dad; they were for the home opener and for anyone in the community.

We'd met baseball players many times before that day. They often came to visit the patients at Oakland Children's Hospital during the off-season. But having them in our town was a whole different experience. They saw where we lived, where we ate, and most importantly, they saw how we treated each other.

With that, the players climbed back into the white van and drove out of town. I will be forever grateful for their visit to our tiny town.

The next few weeks were filled with everything baseball. We were able to go to an A's game at the Oakland Coliseum, and every chance Dad and we kids got, we were in our front yard playing catch, playing games of "pickle," practicing hitting, and running bases. Clint was still very sick, but the thing about cancer is that there are good days and bad days. Thankfully, kids are resilient, and his good days outweighed his bad. He felt well enough to even play on a baseball team that year with our dad as his coach.

Clint may have been dying, but that didn't ever stop him from living.

On Saturday and Sunday afternoons, our family could often be found at Selma Herndon Elementary School, where there was a baseball field complete with bases and a chain-link backstop. It was the perfect place to play a practice game, and where we got in our best practices.

Clint dropped the bat on the grass and ran to first base.

Dad motioned for me to pick up the bat. "Kimmers, it's your turn to hit."

I stood at home plate trying to bend my knees just like I had practiced many times before.

"Keep your eye on the ball," Dad reminded me as he slowly tossed the pitch.

Crack!

The ball sailed between second and third base, and I ran with all my might to first, where Clint was eagerly waiting to tag me out.

Dad scooped up the ball and threw it to Clint.

"Safe!" Dad hollered out as I ran past first base.

The ball landed in Clint's mitt with a smack.

"Good catch," Dad called to Clint. Then to me, "Good run!" He laughed. "You're pretty fast for a girl."

I laughed, too, because Dad had always said that girls could run just as fast as boys.

On that day, we were all having fun playing baseball with some of Clint's friends. Dad was one of the Little League Baseball coaches and loved to get all the kids together to practice as much as possible. Always before they started, Dad let me practice hitting and catching while reminding me of the rules. Not only was Dad there to help teach the kids how to play, but he was getting practice in himself, since he played on a team every chance he got.

The rest of Clint's team arrived, and Mom said, "Okay, let them practice. We can go play somewhere else." Then she added, "Keep your shoes on. Now that the dandelions are blooming there are bees everywhere."

When the weather warmed up, I didn't like wearing shoes. I loved the feel of fresh green grass and dirt between my toes.

Cody, Mom, and I ran across the grass to where the trees nestled close to the classroom buildings so Cody could play in the dirt with his little cars. He and I took turns racing his Hot Wheels in the dirt and over rocks.

The yellow dandelions were calling me, and I left him and Mom to pick flowers. I kicked my shoes off and ran across the grass, picking flowers as I went.

"Ouch!" A stinging pain shot through the bottom of my foot.

Tears rolled down my cheeks when I sat down to look at what was causing so much pain.

"What's wrong?" Mom called.

I was crying too hard to answer her. I had no idea why my foot hurt so bad. She walked over and looked closely at it.

She frowned. "You were stung by a bee, Kimberley, I told you not to take your shoes off."

"I forgot," I wailed.

"You must have stepped on it." She pulled the stinger out of my foot.

I held her hand and hopped on one foot back to my shoes. I carefully put them back on as bees flew around on the grass.

I learned an important lesson that day. When bees are covering the grass, keep your shoes on. I sat in the dirt playing Hot Wheels with Cody, still contemplating my decision about taking my shoes off, when my thoughts were suddenly interrupted.

"Betty!" Dad shouted.

Mom, Cody, and I looked up to see Dad holding his hand over Clint's mouth. Blood was gushing from his face.

Mom picked up Cody and quickly ran to Dad and Clint. I followed close behind them, dragging my aching foot. Mom sprinted to the car and returned with a towel to soak up some of the blood dripping from Clint's face.

Dad hurriedly explained, "Clint tried to catch a fly ball, but it hit him in the face, and he bit his tongue."

Blood was everywhere!

Mom took Clint to the hospital while Cody and I stayed with Dad to finish practice with the rest of Clint's team. Afterward, we got a ride home from one of the parents.

Clint and Mom got home a few hours after us. Clint was holding a large ice pack on his face and couldn't talk very well, but he was in good spirits. Mom explained that doctors weren't able to stitch his tongue, so it would have to heal on its own. She learned that the tongue was the fastest healing organ on the human body, so he should be able to eat and talk like normal within a few days.

Life was always so full of unexpected moments, but none of them ever seemed to faze my big brother. He just rolled with the punches, like he just knew that life would go on.

Spring of 1984, when the Oakland A's came to
our town for a fundraising baseball clinic.

EASTER

A child's imagination can fill their heart
with hope when life tells them otherwise.

~KIMBERLEY'S THOUGHT~

THE DAYS WERE GETTING LONGER, and the Easter holiday was fast approaching. Easter was my favorite holiday because it was usually always on a day that was sunny and warm. I so loved the warm sunshine on my skin.

Easter was also the one day of the year when I was able to wear a new sundress. We only got new clothes twice a year; the beginning of the school year for back-to-school and one outfit for Easter Sunday. Other than that, the rest of Clint's, Cody's, and my clothes were hand-me-downs. I loved being able to dance around in my new dress with the warm sunshine surrounding me. All was right with the world on that day.

"*Here comes Peter Cotton Tail, hopping down the bunny trail. Hippity hop, hippity hop, Easter's on its way…*" Grandma sang out as soon as she saw me walking toward her. She was watering flowers in her front yard. The red camellias that trailed up the side of their yellow house were growing beautifully.

When I got closer, I asked, "Who's Peter Cotton Tail?"

"He's a bunny. He must be friends with the Easter Bunny?" she said thoughtfully.

Now I was excited. "Is the Easter Bunny coming soon?"

"He sure is! You'll need to dye your eggs."

We chatted away while she watered all the plants and flowers in their yard. She told me the names of each one as we moved from one to the next. Grandma loved her flowers, and I grew to love them, too. When all had been watered, she turned off the faucet and wrapped up the hose. "Are you ready for a pudding pop?"

"What's a pudding pop?"

"It's frozen pudding on a stick. It's like a chocolate popsicle."

I followed her to the little house where two upright freezers were plugged in and where the extra food was stored.

The little house was once used as my grandpa's bedroom before he and my grandma were married. It once sat on a cement pad near my great-grandparents' house and was just large enough for his bed and a small dresser. After Grandma and Papa were married, the little house was moved next to their back door and painted yellow to match their main house.

Amongst the thick layers of dust and enormous spider webs, the little house held two freezers along with shelves that housed everything from extra canning jars to Easter baskets. The yellow door was hardly ever closed. An outdoor thermometer was on the outside wall. It was probably one of the most important tools on the entire ranch. It helped my grandpa to know when the grapes needed to be irrigated, or when to prepare for frost. My grandparents often spoke to the outdoor thermometer as if it were alive. I heard more words spoken to that thermometer than any other inanimate object on the ranch.

"Here's one for you, and here's one for me." Grandma handed me what looked like a popsicle with a white wrapper on it.

I carefully held onto the wooden popsicle stick as I peeled the white wrapper off to unveil what looked like frozen chocolate pudding.

"Try it, you'll like it." Grandma took a bite of her own pudding pop.

"Mmm…" I instantly had a new favorite summer treat the moment the pudding pop touched my lips.

I finished eating every last bite of my pudding pop before saying thank you and skipped back to my house. Grandma had reminded me that it was the weekend before Easter, and I could hardly wait to start preparing for it.

We spent the next few days drawing and coloring pictures of all sizes of Easter eggs on construction paper. Then we cut them out and taped them on the windows and walls of our house. By the time Easter arrived, the inside of our house looked like a mosaic of Easter egg construction paper.

The night before Easter was spent dying eggs. Mom covered the entire breakfast bar in newspaper, then took all six of our coffee mugs out of the cupboard and placed them on top of the newspaper.

She told me she'd kept my favorite Swiss Miss mug tucked inside the cupboard so that it wouldn't get stained from egg dye.

I smiled at that gesture, thankful that she realized how much I loved it.

The coffee mugs were all different sizes and colors. My favorite was the little green one, and I instantly claimed it as my own. Clint and I sat on barstools anxiously waiting to see what we were going to do with all of them.

Cody sat wide-eyed on Dad's lap. He looked like he desperately wanted to grab something.

"Don't eat these." Mom handed Clint and me different colored tablets. "Put one in each mug."

We did as instructed, then patiently waited to see what would happen next.

Mom poured something into a glass measuring cup.

"Ugh, what's that smell?" asked Clint.

"It's vinegar. We add this to the tablets to make the egg dye."

We watched in amazement as each tablet fizzed up and slowly disappeared when the vinegar touched them.

"WOW!" we both exclaimed.

Once the fizzing stopped, Mom added water to fill the mugs until they were almost full. She placed a large spoon in each of them, instructing us to stir the concoction around until the colors were bold and bright. Clint and I took pride in being in charge of two mugs each as Dad helped Cody stir the remaining ones.

"Knock, knock," Grandma announced when she and Papa walked into our house. "We're here to help."

"Perfect timing," Clint said. "We're just about to start dying the eggs."

Mom got two dozen hard-boiled eggs out of the fridge and set them on the breakfast bar. She took one out of the carton and showed us how to carefully place it into the mug. Clint and I had dyed eggs before, but since it's something that we only did once a year, it was good to have the reminder of how to do it.

The excitement of Easter filled the air as we spent the next hour dying two dozen eggs in preparation for the Easter Bunny to hide them for us sometime before the sun came up the next morning. We worked hard, turning the white eggs into bright colors. We talked, laughed, and made a huge mess of the breakfast bar.

Once all the white eggs were transformed into Easter eggs, we set each of them on a colorful, round cardboard ring that came with the Paas Easter Egg decorating kit. Mom then transferred all the eggs on their cardboard pedestals to a large glass platter. She set the platter in the middle of the pool table, ensuring us that's where the Easter Bunny would be sure to see them.

Grandma and Papa said their goodbyes as we cleaned up the kitchen and got ready for bed. Once we were in our pajamas, we went back into the living room. Mom was sitting in one of the gold chairs with a book in her hand. "It's time to read an Easter story."

Cody climbed up onto her lap while Clint and I sat at her feet. Page by page, she read a story about the Easter Bunny who was trying to find all the hidden eggs.

"Where does the Easter Bunny live?" I asked.

"In the swamp!" Dad called from the family room.

We all laughed at that answer.

I was confused. "What's a swamp?"

Mom flipped through the book and showed us a picture of the Easter Bunny looking for an Easter egg in a swamp. "Like this."

Seeing the picture made us all laugh even harder.

Clint insisted that the Easter Bunny lived in a cave in the forest.

Cody, who was just learning how to talk, interjected something that didn't make much sense to any of us.

Mom gave a few suggestions of where the Easter Bunny might live, but I really had no idea, so the swamp made just as much sense to me as anyplace else.

Mom finished reading the story, then shuffled us all off to bed.

As soon as Clint and I climbed into our beds, his nose started to bleed. Without saying a word, he climbed down the ladder and went to the bathroom for some toilet paper.

I lay in my own bed wondering if he'd need to go to the hospital that night, and we would spend Easter Sunday in the hospital. Would the Easter Bunny find us there? It had been a busy week preparing for Easter, so sleep came much quicker than normal that night. So many thoughts stirred inside my head as I slowly drifted off to sleep; I don't remember Clint coming back to bed.

Thump!

I felt the whole house shake and woke up to what I was sure must be the Easter Bunny.

"Clint, what was *that*?"

Thankfully he answered me, "I don't know."

We both got out of our beds and looked out the window, but we couldn't see anything except a dark sky and the dim light illuminating from the dusk-to-dawn light that stood near the Quonset hut. Everything always seemed scarier in the darkness of night.

"Maybe we should go ask Mom and Dad," Clint suggested.

We slowly tiptoed through the house until we made it into Mom and Dad's bedroom.

Mom sat up. "What's the matter?"

"What was that noise?" I asked.

"What noise?"

I explained, "It was a loud thump, and the whole house shook."

"I didn't hear anything. Maybe it was an earthquake," said Mom.

I shook my head. "I don't think so." By that point in my young life, I had felt many earthquakes, and I was positive that it wasn't an earthquake. "It was like someone really heavy was jumping in the house. I think it was the Easter Bunny!" I grinned.

"Maybe. I didn't hear or feel anything. It might just be your mind playing tricks on you." Mom smiled. "You kids go back to bed."

Clint and I went back into our room. I climbed up the ladder behind him, deciding I would sleep up there until it was time to get up. We talked about all kinds of things, including what else the noise could have possibly been besides the Easter Bunny. We never came up with an answer and finally settled on the fact that we'd probably never know for sure. We were still talking when the darkness in the sky turned lighter with each passing moment.

Finally, we decided that it was officially Easter morning, so we snuck into Cody's room to see if he was awake. To our delight he was, so Clint lifted him out of his crib, and then the three of us ran into the living room to see if the Easter Bunny had left us anything.

Sitting in the middle of the room were three Easter baskets. Each woven plastic basket was a different color. One green and white, a pink and white, and a yellow and white one. Each basket was filled with green Easter grass, small toys, and candy. We were still staring at them when Mom and Dad walked into the room.

"Go ahead, see what the Easter Bunny left for you," said Dad.

We each took a basket and carefully pulled out the goodies, observing each one closely. We were thrilled that the Easter Bunny had brought us so many wonderful treats. We each got a chocolate bunny, marshmallow eggs, a small green plastic water gun, Silly Putty, water balloons, and a deck of cards. In no time at all, we were chewing the ears off our chocolate bunnies, and our faces were covered in chocolate.

The rest of the day was a blur of looking for Easter eggs, going to church, playing with our new water guns, water balloon fights with our cousins, and having a barbeque at our grandparents' house. I had forgotten all about Clint's bloody nose the night before, but I was thankful that we didn't have to spend the day at the hospital. I was able to twirl around in my new sundress the whole day while using my new pink and white Easter basket to look for eggs on multiple hunts.

That night, I lay in our bedroom thinking about the perfect day. I was looking at the new painting Mom hung on our wall at the end of my bed.

It was a colorful painting of a young boy and girl picking flowers near a small stream in the forest. She painted it with Tri-Chem paints. The different bold shades of blues, greens, and browns lit up the room. When the bedroom was dark, certain spots of the painting glowed.

I lay there that night looking with fascination at the glowing parts of that painting. The trees, the grass, the rocks, and the pretty blue stream all slowly disappeared into the darkness. Only the young boy and girl, the flowers, and something new were visible now. Up in the left-hand corner was the face of Jesus watching over the two children. A face that was only visible when it was really dark in our bedroom; Jesus. I wondered if he could always see us in the darkness like that. It brought both fear and joy to my heart. It was a little scary to think of someone watching me while I slept. But then I thought about Clint. He had mentioned seeing Jesus before, and he always lit up with excitement when he talked about that incident. Maybe I had nothing to be fearful of. I pondered those thoughts as I fell asleep staring at Jesus' glowing face.

SUMMER

Summer sunshine is medicine for the soul.

~KIMBERLEY'S THOUGHT~

Late spring soon turned into early summer, my favorite time of year. The huge vegetable garden behind my great-grandparents' house was filled with a variety of plants: zucchini, cucumbers, radishes, and rows and rows of tomatoes that were just starting to bud. It would make for a plentiful summer harvest come June, July, and August.

At the end of the garden was a large pile of firewood that would soon be stacked in long rows in preparation for winter. The woodpile was the perfect place for Clint and me to look for lizards. The first time I tried to catch one, I pulled him by the tail, and it fell right off! I was sure that I'd killed him and felt horrible about it. Thankfully, that was short-lived because Mom explained to me that the lizard was perfectly fine, and that its tail would soon grow back.

Besides picking vegetables from the garden and catching lizards, summer was the time of birthday celebrations, playing outside, irrigation, hiding in grapevines, swimming, taking long walks, and so much more. The first summer birthday was Clint's, which was always a big deal. Every birthday was an important milestone for him because doctors never expected him to live to see even his fifth birthday, making each year that he grew older a miracle.

We were all preparing for the celebration when talk of his birthday the year before came up. There were a few unexpected twists to it that we still can't believe all occurred simultaneously.

"Do you remember your birthday party last year?" Mom asked Clint.

"Yeah, that was crazy."

Mom had become quite a cake designer over the years. She baked and designed elaborate cakes for the birthdays of close friends and family members. Each year, we kids were able to choose the design we wanted, and she put that plan into action.

That year, Dad had been extra busy with fire calls with the Livingston Fire Department, so Clint chose to have a fire scene on his cake, complete with burning buildings. Mom spent hours working on creating the perfect birthday cake for him, and we couldn't wait to see how it turned out.

Clint had a few of his closest friends over for his party. The moment had come for Mom to light the candles while we sang Happy Birthday. She set the cake on the breakfast bar, lit the little buildings on fire first to stage the special effects, then she lit the candles. We all started singing.

"*Happy Birthday to you, Happy Birthday to you, Happy Birthday Dear Clint...*"

"Earthquake!" Mom shouted.

The whole house started shaking. One of Clint's friends ran and hid under the pool table. Mom and Dad blew out the candles and extinguished the burning buildings on the cake. The rest of us ran outside.

We'd experienced earthquakes many times before, so we knew the drill—run outside and stand in the middle of the yard so nothing could hit us. Mom and Dad convinced Clint's friend under the pool table to run outside, too.

We stayed there for a few minutes to ensure that the shaking had stopped, then Dad's beeper went off. The strong 6.2 Coalinga earthquake had caused problems somewhere in town that he needed to help with.

Dad hurried off while the rest of us spent the remainder of Clint's birthday experiencing aftershock after aftershock while trying to eat a piece of his cake and watching him open presents. It was definitely a celebration to remember.

"I don't think we can make your birthday that exciting this year." Mom laughed.

"So, no fire on my birthday cake?"

"No! No fire!"

Clint agreed to have something other than burning buildings on his cake and continued making birthday party plans; it came and went without a hitch. It was not quite as memorable as the year before, but it was just as special. He had stayed alive for another year, and that was reason enough to celebrate.

Following Clint's birthday were the last few weeks of school. Dad was the newly appointed fire chief, and one day he showed up with the firetruck at the kindergarten playground. He was joined by a few other volunteer firefighters to teach us all about fire safety. They taught us how to stop, drop, and roll, how to use a fire extinguisher, and how to smother a small fire with a blanket or a jacket. At one point, they dressed fully in their fire gear, with face masks and all, carrying us one by one across the playground to the other side. They did that to demonstrate how not to be afraid of a firefighter if they came to rescue us in a burning building.

Why would we be afraid of a firefighter?

I patiently waited in line for my turn. A good friend was in front of me, and I watched as my dad carried her from the sidewalk where we were standing to the chain-link fence across from us. I thought for sure that he would hurry back for me, but he didn't. Instead, I was picked up by a different firefighter. For a second, I actually was a little scared as the smell of wood smoke emitted from the tall man's yellow heavy turnout coat.

"It's just me." I could hear the man say in a muffled voice through his face mask. He pointed to his eyes, which were covered with eyeglasses and a clear face shield. I quickly realized that I knew who the firefighter was who was holding me. It was our good family friend, Gary. I instantly relaxed as he carried me over to where my friends were. He set me down and ruffled my head before returning to the other side of the playground.

After all of us kids were safely moved, the firefighters let us take turns holding the firehose that was hooked up to the water tanker. We squealed with excitement when water sprayed all over the playground by the big trees. Fire could be scary but learning about how to be safe around it and how to put it out was a lot of fun.

Dad picked me up in a big hug before he and the other fire crew members got in their firetrucks and drove away. That was one of my most memorable days of kindergarten.

Before long, the school year came to an end. I said goodbye to my kindergarten teacher, my friends, and even the lunch card lady, not really understanding that it would be months before I'd see most of them again. I also didn't fully understand that I'd never be in the same classroom with the same group of friends, nor that I'd never be able to play on the giant silver metal teeter-totters at recess.

Life is funny like that; not knowing until after things are over that they will never again be the same.

In the mix of the school year coming to an end, I celebrated my sixth birthday. It was the day that I wore my little red kindergarten dress for one of the very last times. It was a special dress that Mom had let me pick out of the Sears Catalog a few weeks before

I started school that year. It was the first time in my life that I'd looked through pages and pages of colored pictures of clothes in the catalog, trying to decide on a new outfit for myself. When I'd finally settled on claiming the little red dress as my own, I then had to wait weeks for it to arrive in the mail. It made it to our house just in time for me to wear it for the first day of kindergarten.

It was a short red dress with tiny white daisies all over it. I wore it with pride as often as I could, with my matching sandals. Even in the cold winter months, I would wear it with white tights so I would be warm. I wore that dress until the day came when it no longer fit. Lucky for me, I didn't grow very fast, so I was able to wear my kindergarten dress the whole year, all the way to my sixth birthday.

That year, I had a small party, and I happily pranced around in my little red dress with some of my closest friends. Instead of one of Mom's fancy cakes, I asked her to make me an ice cream dessert. She made the cutest little ice cream cone clowns and surprised me with them during my party. It was the best sixth birthday party a girl could ask for.

Birthday celebrations were special but summer was also when my brothers and I spent a lot of time having fun playing in the dirt. We'd spend hours building sandcastles and having dirt clod fights in the furrows behind the house. Dodging dirt clods was just as much fun as throwing them. Though the fights usually ended with frustration because one of us had sand in our eyes. So, we would dust ourselves off and head back in the house to clean up.

The dirt on the ranch was a unique sandy soil that was particularly fertile. It was ideal for growing a variety of crops but also special for making great sandcastles. Mom taught us how to get the soil wet enough to slowly drip through our fingers, which allowed it to plop on the sand, forming the pillars for our castles. Drop by drop, we soon created masterpieces. As they dried, they could be shaped with sticks to form clean edges for the walls, doorways, and windows. We'd sometimes even have contests for who could build the biggest, smallest, prettiest, ugliest, or whatever other castle design we could conjure up. Sometimes we'd make them big enough to drive our Hot Wheels cars into. The possibilities were endless.

We walked into the house covered in dirt after a busy day of making sand castles and having a brutal dirt clod battle.

Dad asked, "Who wants to go and check the water with me?"

My hand shot up. "Me!"

"Okay, go get in the truck."

Irrigation time was a rotation of stressful weeks all summer long. It had to be done throughout the summer to ensure the grapevines were getting enough water to keep them well hydrated in the scorching Central Valley heat. With temperatures rising into the hundred-degree mark, it was important that all one hundred twenty acres of grapes were thoroughly watered. Papa took care of the irrigating during the day, and Dad oversaw the evening and nighttime irrigating.

I ran from the house to the 1970s light blue Ford work truck and climbed into the passenger side. The smell of dust, leather seats, and country living consumed my senses as I waited for Dad to climb into the driver's side. He checked to make sure his shovel was in the truck bed, then climbed in and started the engine. He drove from its parking spot between our house and my grandparents' house to the dirt road that led to the field. We chatted away as he drove past each row, checking to see that the water was making its way down the furrows.

Dad put the truck in park, climbed out, and grabbed his shovel. "The water isn't where it should be on this row."

I jumped out and followed close behind him. Our three dogs had joined us and trotted along beside me.

He dug around the area where the water seemed to be stopped.

"What do you think is wrong, Dad?"

He shrugged. "Might be gophers."

Evening soon turned to night, and it was too dark for him to see where he was shoveling, so we went back to the truck to get the lantern. The little mesh mantels were enclosed in glass and made a poof sound when the match ignited them.

Dad handed it to me. "Be careful not to burn yourself."

I slowly swung it back and forth, watching the light flicker as we walked back.

When we got back to the water, I set the green lantern down on the mound of dirt in the middle of two furrows.

Dad began shoveling by the lantern light, and my stomach growled.

"I'm hungry."

"I know, but we can't leave until this water is moving along like it should." He sounded a little stressed. "See that stick over there?" He motioned to a long stick on the ground.

"Yeah."

"See if you can use it to help me get this water moving."

"Okay." I picked up the stick, put it into the water, and gave it a sweeping motion. "Like this?"

His voice lifted. "I think that's working. It must be a magic stick."

I beamed with joy thinking that I was really helping my dad to fix the irrigation problem.

Dad smiled, and his stress seemed to disappear as he watched me move my "magic stick" back and forth. He then shoveled for a long time while I "helped" him with my magic stick.

Finally, the water was flowing like it was supposed to.

"I think things are all set here. Bring the lantern. We'll walk ahead a little way to make sure it's all fixed."

I walked behind him swinging the lantern.

"Ouch!" I screamed.

Dad spun around. "What happened?"

I sputtered, "The lantern…burned my arm…" Tears rolled down my cheeks.

"I told you to be careful," he gently reminded me.

"I forgot." I set the lantern on the dirt.

Dad walked over to where I was standing and tenderly took my arm in his hands. "That's a pretty good burn you've got. That's going to blister. Here, put some water on it."

He bent down and helped me put my arm in the cool running water trickling down the furrow. We sat there for a few minutes until the initial sting from the burn dissipated.

He picked up the lantern and his shovel and started walking toward the truck.

I walked as close to him as I could, blowing cool air on my burned arm.

Once we got to the truck, Dad set the lantern on the tailgate and extinguished the flame. He put it where it wouldn't break, then we climbed in the truck and started for home.

We were riding comfortably in the dark, talking about the burn on my arm, when Dad suddenly slammed on the brakes, and I lurched forward.

A young cottontail rabbit stood in the road right in front of us, blinded by the truck's headlights.

Our dogs, Ringo, Banjo, and Ranger, who had been running behind us, caught up to us and ran in front of the truck.

The truck's headlights shone brightly on them as Ranger sank his teeth into the little cottontail and held it in his mouth.

"Oh no!" I yelled.

The desperate rabbit squealed.

Dad jumped out of the truck and hollered for Ranger to drop

the cottontail. The dog instantly dropped the rabbit onto the dirt and watched over it like a statue.

Dad picked it up; it was still alive, so he placed it on a red rag on the seat. He gently petted it. "I think it might just be in shock."

We both got back into the truck.

"Can I hold it?"

"Scoot over and I'll give it to you."

I slid next to Dad, and he gently placed the rag and rabbit on my lap. He put the truck in gear, and we again headed for home.

The rabbit was breathing heavier and heavier giving me an icky feeling inside. Tears welled up in my eyes. "Daddy, I think this little rabbit is going to die." I petted the rabbit's soft fur.

"He might be bleeding internally. Try saying a little prayer for it. That might help."

"Lord Jesus, please help save this baby rabbit's life," I pleaded. "He's so cute, and his brown fur is so soft. Look at how soft his tail is." But the prayer didn't help. I felt the cottontail go completely limp and die in my arms before we made it to the house.

"He died, Daddy. He's dead. Why does everything have to die?" Big tears streamed down my face.

Dad and I were quiet for the rest of the ride home. When we finally made it to our house, Dad parked the truck at the end of our sidewalk.

"Here, Pumpkin, I'll take it. We can bury him or her under the plum tree tomorrow." He carefully took the rabbit from my arms and wrapped it in the rag.

I was too upset to see what Dad did with the rabbit. I jumped out of the truck and walked to the house scuffing my feet all the way, tears rolling down my cheeks.

I walked in through the sliding door.

Mom took one look at me. "What's the matter?"

"The rabbit died," I said, completely downtrodden.

She stretched her arms out. "Come here." She embraced me in a hug.

Mom was probably thoroughly confused as to what had transpired with a rabbit, but I was too upset to explain it to her.

Dad came in shortly after and explained the whole ordeal to her.

After Dad finished explaining, I couldn't hold back my frustration any longer. I was mad. "It was Ranger's fault!" I pointed outside where I knew the dogs were.

"He was just doing what dogs do. They chase and kill smaller animals—like rabbits," Dad reminded me.

"And rabbits carry diseases, so you really need to go and wash your hands. In fact, you need to go and take a bath. You're filthy." Mom pointed out as I slowly walked toward the bathroom. "And don't forget to wash behind your ears!" she reminded me.

I always forgot to wash behind my ears.

Irrigation time often made for late dinners, long nights, and lots of unexpected and stressful situations. That's just how life was on the ranch, regardless of whether my brother was dying of cancer or not. The older I grew, the more I began to realize that each day carried a weight all its own. The death of the rabbit made me completely forget about the burn on my arm. I did put ice on it the next morning to help ease the pain, but it still blistered up just like Dad said it would. Looking at Jesus lit up on the painting, I cried myself to sleep that night, wondering why he let things die.

That day I learned a lesson about lantern safety that I shared with anyone who would listen. The blister was there for a week or more before it finally popped and left a dark brown scab. I carried the lantern many more times after that night, but I never swung it back and forth again. I always set it down, picked it up, and carried it very carefully. I was never scared of the lantern, though, because it's what brought us light in the darkness, and light brought me joy.

Me in my red dress on the first day of kindergarten 1983.

22

KENNEDY MEADOWS

~KIMBERLEY'S THOUGHT~

AS THE GRAPES MATURED on the vines and irrigation came to an end, Dad and Papa were able to relax for a few days. Camping and fishing is how they liked to spend their downtime. At the beginning of every summer, my grandparents hauled their trailer up to Kennedy Meadows Resort and Pack Station to a special reserved spot and kept it there the entire summer. They took any chance there was to escape from the Central Valley for a day or two. This campsite was at the base of the Sonora Pass in the Sierra Nevada Mountains. In fact, they spent so much time there every year, that on their sixtieth anniversary the staff took a picture of them sitting on a rock near the cabins. It was placed on the wall in the Kennedy Meadows bar and remains there to this day.

I was only two weeks old the first time my parents took me camping at Kennedy's, so I never knew what it was like not to camp there. Grandma and Papa's campsite was along the edge of Deadman Creek and became one of my most favorite places on

Earth. The creek was filled with large boulders that made for great stepping stones when trying to get to the perfect fishing holes. The water was fast-moving, and large pine trees along the banks shaded the creek in just the right amount of darkness all summer long. The trees were home to chipmunks, squirrels, and birds that made their presence known throughout each day. The chipmunks weren't the least bit shy and spent much of their day eating a peanut or two from my grandparents' campsite.

Kennedy's was a special place for our family for a variety of reasons. One of them being that it was where my parents met. I heard the story so many times about their meeting that I began to feel as if I was actually there when it happened.

When she was eleven years old, Mom was camping at Kennedy's with her parents and sisters. The family was on their annual two-week camping trip when she first saw Dad.

She was fishing from the bank when on the other side of the river, a cute boy and his friend caught her eye. That same day, she saw that boy again; he and his dad were visiting with my grandparents at their campsite. They had come from San Francisco to Kennedy's to stay in a cabin for the weekend. While everyone was visiting, Mimi and Bompa showed up with my grandparents' mail. Seeing their address, Grandpa Ghiggia asked Grandma and Papa Pierce about bird hunting on their property in the Central Valley. From there, a kinship grew between the two families. The cute boy, Dad, was thirteen years old at the time and began writing letters to Mom, as well as taking frequent hunting trips to the ranch with Grandpa Ghiggia.

Thankfully, the summer of 1984 wasn't much different than any other summer of my childhood. Any chance we could, my family took several quick overnight or two-day trips to Kennedy's. We also spent every weekend possible on other camping and fishing excursions in both California and Nevada. When we ventured to other places, we always discovered something new. A fishing spot, hiking trail, or a dirt road to drive down.

Kennedy's was different, though, because it was more like home. It wasn't an adventure; it was a place of calm, healing, and familiarity, to escape the chaos of life. It was the perfect place to retreat from busy ranch work, the big city hospital, and doctor visits.

I was sitting in the dirt between the river and my grandparents' campsite looking at rocks when my brothers walked up with Dad.

Clint asked, "Do you want to go to the store with us?"

"Yes," I said absently. I was carefully analyzing a rock.

Grandma had been watching me from the picnic table. "That's granite, Kimmy."

"What's granite?"

She chuckled. "It's that rock that you're holding. See how it's white with black speckles? It's pretty, isn't it?"

"Yes, it's really pretty."

Mom joined me. "It's volcanic."

"Wow!" I was trying to understand exactly what that even meant.

"It's everywhere around here. These mountains are full of granite," said Papa.

"It is? This kind of rock is everywhere?" I held my breath a little as I thought about the mountains surrounding me being filled with such beautiful rocks.

"It's just a rock, Kim. Are you going to walk to the store with us or not?" Clint impatiently walked out of the campsite in the direction of the camp store.

"Yes, I'm coming." I stood and walked over to the picnic table. I set the rock down but hesitated.

Papa laughed. "We'll make sure that it stays right there until you get back."

Dad was carrying Cody; he and Clint were already walking up the dirt road in the direction of the store, so I had to run to catch up with them.

Almost out of breath, I grabbed Dad's hand. "Can we get ice cream?"

Dad swung my arm back and forth as we walked. "Sure, that's what we're going for."

Tall pine trees towered above us on both sides of the dirt road, the scent of fresh pine surrounded us. The river to our right roared along its path, and the small wood cabins on our left were filled with weekend visitors hauling things to and from their vehicles.

Dad looked in that direction. "I used to help clean those."

"You did?" I asked.

"Yeah, when I was a teenager. I came up for the summer to help clean the cabins and take care of the horses."

"Was it fun?"

Clint scowled. "Doesn't sound like fun to me."

Dad laughed. "It was a lot of work, but yeah, it was fun, too."

We walked past the cabins, a huge boulder, and the cabins where the staff stayed. We turned left when we got to the big green lodge with a sign that read, "WELCOME TO KENNEDY MEADOWS."

We walked past the laundry, the bathrooms that looked more like outhouses, and the smell of horse manure greeted us when we got closer to the corals.

Clint looked puzzled. "Dad, I thought we were going to the store? I want to see Millie."

"We are, but I wanted to stop and see the horses first."

"There aren't very many here," I said.

"No, most of them are out on pack trips right now."

Clint and I petted a few of the horses while Dad, still holding Cody in his arms, visited with one of the cowboys. We walked toward the lodge and went in through the back door. We said our hellos to the people who worked there, then went through the lobby. The smell of bacon filled the air from the nearby restaurant. We went out the front door and down the stairs. Finally, we turned left, walked past the pay phone, and opened the screen door to enter the store.

"Hi, Millie!" we all said at the same time.

Millie was standing behind the counter "Hi, y'all!" She turned to Clint. "How are you feeling?"

Clint touched his head. "I'm good. I lost all my hair again, but it's starting to grow back."

"Well, I think you look great!" She smiled. "It's so good to see all of you!" She motioned toward the wall across from her. "Get yourselves some ice cream."

Dad opened the white chest freezer filled with ice cream. Clint and I each picked out a Root Beer Float Bar, and Dad chose an Ice Cream Sandwich. He also grabbed a Root Beer Float Bar for Mom. We paid fifty cents each for our treats, said our goodbyes to Millie, then left the store.

Clint and I opened our Root Beer Float Bars as quickly as we could and devoured them as we walked back to the campsite.

"Do you guys want to go for a walk to the meadow in a little while?" asked Dad.

"Yes!" I shouted out between bites.

"I'm not sure yet," said Clint. "I might stay at camp and play darts with Grandma and Jerry."

We used to call Papa Jerry, before Cody changed it to Papa.

"Are you feeling bad, Clint?" I asked.

"I'm okay, just a little tired. How far are you going to walk?" Clint asked Dad.

"I don't know. We'll take our fishing poles and walk the river. We'll probably make it as far as the first bridge, but with Cody, it will be too hard to go all the way to the second bridge."

Clint shook his head. "Nah, you guys go ahead. Walking to the first bridge sounds really far today. I'll just hang out with Grandma and Jerry."

"Okay, you can always fish in Deadman with Jerry if you feel up to it."

"Yeah, I'll probably do that."

"Can we roast marshmallows when we get back from our hike?" I asked.

Dad sighed. "Is that all you think about is food?"

I giggled. "I guess."

Clint laughed and announced, "We're back!" as we walked into camp.

"They made it!" called Grandma.

"Here you go, Boop." Dad set Cody in a lawn chair and handed Mom her Root Beer Float Bar. "Clint's going to stay here while we hike to the meadow. Is that okay with you guys?"

"Of course," said Grandma.

"Sure. I'll teach him how to fish." Papa chuckled.

Mom, Dad, Cody, and I spent the rest of the day hiking all the way to the meadow and fishing along the river and to the first bridge. When we got there, Mom and Dad searched for where they had carved their initials when they were teenagers. It was always exciting to see that it was still there. We caught two fish that day and carried them back to camp to eat for dinner. Rainbow trout wrapped in aluminum foil always tasted amazingly delicious when cooked over the fire with a little lemon, butter, and garlic.

After dinner, Dad got out his guitar and strummed it as we sat around the campfire singing songs. We belted out the words to the songs "Where Have All the Flowers Gone?" and "Tom Dooley" while we roasted marshmallows over the fire. We tried to sing "Kumbaya," but I couldn't quite get through all the lines of it because the sugar from the marshmallows had kicked in, and I needed to do something other than sing.

I moved around restlessly in the aluminum lawn chair. "Can we do something else?"

"Someone's getting squirmy." Papa threw another log on the fire.

"Let's play charades!" said Clint.

"Yeah!" I shouted.

"How about we have teams?" Mom suggested. "Kimmy, Cody, and I against the rest of you."

The old lodge at Kennedy Meadows

Photo taken by Betty Pierce 1966

"It's a deal. We're going to win!" Clint jumped up. "I'll go first." He motioned the signal with his arms that he'd be acting out a movie, and we all started guessing which one he was thinking of.

"Remember, no talking and no sounds," Mom reminded him as he started making shooting sounds.

After several rounds of charades, the fire started to die down. We sat in folding chairs and looked up at the stars. Our eyes became heavy while Mom, Dad, and Papa pointed out the different constellations.

"Let's get our sleeping bags," said Dad. He and Mom put our bags out on a blue tarp close to my grandparents' trailer.

Mom put Cody in his playpen while Clint and I grabbed the pillows out of the car and set them at the head of our sleeping bags. It didn't take long before we were all changed into our pajamas and ready for bed.

I knew there was always the chance that a black bear might walk right up to us while we were sleeping, but that thought didn't bother me at all. Sleeping outside was special, and I couldn't have imagined anything better than falling asleep under the light of the crescent moon and twinkling stars as I crawled into my bag.

FOURTH OF JULY

CAMPING AND FISHING were important parts of our summer, but there's nothing that represented summer being in full swing quite like fireworks. As the days grew closer and closer to the Fourth of July, my parents had slowly started stockpiling sparklers, firecrackers, and the fireworks called Ground Bloom Flowers and Black Snakes. My favorite were the Black Snakes because they didn't make any loud noises. I have highly sensitive hearing, and sometimes the loud booms of the fireworks scared me to my core.

Mom was busy planting marigolds near the tomato plants in the garden.

"When are we going to see fireworks?" I asked.

"Not for a few more days. Why don't you come and help me in the garden?"

"What can I do?"

"You can help me water the plants, pick all of the tomatoes off the vines, and search for worms. We need to find all the little pests so they'll stop eating the tomatoes!"

"Clint and I found a lot of them in the garden by Mimi and Bompa's house yesterday."

"I'm sure. They have a big garden this year with lots of tomato plants."

"Yeah, they have lots of radishes, too."

"I know. I'm so happy because I love radishes."

Mom and I worked together for the next hour picking green juicy tomato worms off the plants and putting them into a bucket. We picked big, ripe red tomatoes, and watered the garden beds in our front yard.

After Mom seemed to have had enough of my help, I ran off to see what Papa was doing in the Quonset. My bare feet carried me from our warm sidewalk to the hot sandy soil. As I got closer, I could hear talking and hammering, so I picked up my speed to see what was happening inside. I turned too sharply, slamming my right foot into the pile of rocks that sat at the base of the dusk-to-dawn light.

As pain shot from my big toe all the way up my leg. I could hear Papa's voice in my head,

You need to go and put some shoes on. You're going to stub your toe one of these days if you keep walking around barefoot everywhere.

He'd told me that so many times, it was as if the words had no meaning at all. Yet there I was, his words had come true. It was almost as if he made me stub my toe.

"Ouch!" I squealed and reached down to grab my big toe in hopes that it would make the shooting pain go away. I squeezed it, and blood oozed out all sides of my dangling toenail, and the rocks were splattered with blood.

I sat there for a few minutes, contemplating whether I should limp back to my house or just stay there in hopes someone would come and find me.

Nope, this is my fault for not wearing shoes. I need to be strong

and not cry. I need to prove that it's okay to not wear shoes.

I stood up as tall as I could and walked toward the opening of the Quonset. I decided to pretend as if nothing had happened at all.

Papa and Clint walked out just as I was walking in.

Clint looked down. "What happened to your foot?"

"Looks like you stubbed your toe," Papa said.

There it is, the infamous, you're going to stub your toe one of these days, coming true.

"I'll bet that hurts. You'll wear shoes next time, won't you?" I heard love and sympathy in Papa's chuckle. "Come on, let's go to the house and clean it up. I'm going to have to cut that toenail off." He took my hand, leading me to his house, with Clint walking beside me.

"What happened?" Grandma asked right when we walked in the door.

"Oh,…this dumb little kid just stubbed her toe. I tried to tell her to wear shoes, but she didn't want to listen. She's as stubborn as her mom," Papa said as if he was proud that he'd known it was going to happen.

I went into the bathroom and sat down on the closed toilet lid while Papa opened bathroom cupboards and drawers looking for everything he'd need to doctor me up. He scrubbed his hands as if he were preparing for surgery. Once he thoroughly washed, he turned toward me.

"It's raining!" He laughed as he flicked the water from his hands to cover my face with little water droplets.

"You got me all wet." I laughed, holding back tears.

"I did? Well, how did that happen?"

Papa's "it's raining" scenario had been played out many times before that moment so I was prepared for the water droplets to fly in my direction.

Clint and Grandma stood in the bathroom doorway, watching the whole scene unfold. I continued to hold in my tears to try and prove my toughness as Papa held my big toe in his hand and examined it closer. He dabbed it with a wet washcloth until most of the blood was wiped away. Then, he reached for a pair of shiny silver clippers off the bathroom counter.

"This is going to hurt, but just for a second." He quickly cut my toenail completely off in one snip.

Grandma handed him a piece of gauze and a roll of white athletic tape, and before I knew it, my toe was all taped up and looked like a giant marshmallow.

"There, it will do for now. Your mom can clean it up better later. Your toenail should start growing back in a year or two."

My eyes shot open as wide as they could go. "A year or two?"

"Probably in a few weeks, Kimmy. You'll be fine. Jerry's just pulling your leg." Grandma reassured me.

"Now go home and put some shoes on." Papa chuckled as he scooted Clint and me out the door.

"How'd you do that?" Clint asked as we walked home.

"I was running and wasn't watching where I was going. I hit it right here on this rock." I pointed it out as we stopped to examine the scene of the incident before we got to our house.

"Mom's probably going to put that red spray on your big toe later." Clint's comment made my whole body shiver.

That red spray always hurt worse than any cut, burn, or sliver ever did. I hated that spray. Maybe I could just hide my toe from her so that she'd never know it was hurt.

I could hear Willie Nelson belting out tunes from a vinyl record on the stereo as we walked up the steps to our front porch. I looked down at my big toe, wondering how I could hide it from Mom.

Mom was busy playing with Cody in the living room, so I was safe for the time being. She was chasing Cody through the plastic white tunnel that Santa had brought us. It actually ended up being mostly his.

"Kimmy stubbed her toe," Clint belted out as soon as we rounded the pool table in the family room.

Out of breath, Mom said, "That was bound to happen. Let me see it." She crawled out of the plastic tunnel.

I walked over to her and held my foot up like a strong and sturdy soldier without a tear in my eyes.

How did everyone know that I was going to stub my toe? It's like it had been written on my forehead or something. Maybe since she'd known it was going to happen, she wouldn't put that awful red spray on it.

"Who bandaged it up for you?"

"Papa."

"He did a good job."

And with that, she went back to playing with Cody.

Phew, maybe it wouldn't need the red spray after all.

I went to my bedroom to look for my tennis shoes and sandals. I'd need to have them for the next time I went outside to play.

After dinner that night, and after I'd watched the show *Emergency*, we all went for a walk down the field to watch the sunset. I tried to put my tennis shoes on before we left the house, but the bandage on my big toe was too big to fit.

Mom and Dad both suggested that I just go barefoot, but I didn't want to chance stubbing another toe, so I insisted on wearing shoes of some kind. Finally, after much discussion, Dad helped me put my white sandals on.

"Let's look for doodlebugs," Mom said as we walked down the dirt road with rows and rows of grapevines on each side of us.

I looked up at her. "What are doodlebugs?"

"They're the bugs that we look for every summer. You remember? The ones that make doodle marks like this." She pointed to lines that looked like they had been drawn. She bent down and filled her hand with dirt. She shook some of the dirt away and asked me, "Can you see the little doodlebug moving around?" She brushed the rest of the dirt away from her hand to reveal a little gray bug moving in her palm.

"Ooh, he tickles. Do you want to hold him?" She held her hand close to me and slowly slid the tiny bug into my hand.

"Ooooo…he does tickle." The little bug squirmed around.

I set him back on the ground and looked around for other doodle marks. I wanted to find a doodlebug of my own. Clint, Mom, and I found several more before realizing that Dad and Cody were several yards ahead of us. We scrambled to catch up with them before they got to the end of the road.

Once we caught up to them, the five of us walked together and watched the sun set behind the Coast Range Mountains. The sky turned golden orange and pale yellow with shades of pink. The colors blended so well together that it looked as if someone had painted the whole sky with watercolors. I wondered how a sky that was so blue during the day could change to look so different right before it got dark each night.

Mom took a deep breath and sighed. "It's so beautiful tonight."

"It really is pretty, Boop." Dad agreed.

They stood close to each other and held hands as they stared at the sky. I looked at them and then looked up again. I couldn't decide what I loved more at that moment; my family, the sunset, or the fact that the night sky would be filled with fireworks in just a few more days.

After the sun had fully set, we walked back down the dusty road and headed for home. Before we reached the house, the first stars of the night started to twinkle. We stopped in the middle of the road and looked for more stars until the sky turned completely dark.

"Should we have a lantern or a flashlight?" I asked, suddenly realizing how dark it was.

Clint pointed ahead. "The house is just right there."

"I can't see it."

"But we know it's right there."

"Besides, we don't need artificial light. The stars are the map of the sky. Sailors use them to find their way across the sea at night. Surely, we can use them to find our way home if we need to," said Mom.

"How?"

"Do you see that star right there?" Dad pointed to the brightest star in the sky.

"Yeah."

"Well, if you stare at it long enough, it will fall out of the sky and land right on our house. That's called a falling star." He laughed, picked me up, and tickled me until I was laughing so hard I couldn't even breathe. I wondered for a second if that was true as I glanced back toward the sky to see if that really bright star was still there.

The five of us spent the rest of our walk home telling silly stories, looking for constellations, and laughing. Long evening walks in the summertime were the best form of entertainment on the ranch.

Before I knew it, it was finally the Fourth of July, America's birthday. Clint, Cody, Dad, and I spent the whole day playing football and baseball in our front yard and lighting off snakes and flowers.

Mom spent most of the day getting ready for the afternoon barbeque by baking a cake and preparing the rest of the food that we'd be eating later.

"When do we get to go and see fireworks?" I asked.

Dad laughed. "Not until it gets dark. It has to be night to see the fireworks light up the sky, silly."

Soon we could smell the BBQ chicken cooking on Papa's black barbecue grill. We helped Mom carry the food from our house to Grandma and Papa's front yard. We set everything on the picnic table that my Uncle Randall had built for Papa for Father's Day. Grandma had covered it with a festive red and white plastic tablecloth so that we didn't spill anything on the wood. It was filled with watermelon, barbequed chicken, potato salad, hot dogs, green salad, sliced tomatoes, and so much more.

The flies and mosquitoes were swarming everywhere, so Grandma covered each dish with a white foldable mesh tent.

"There, that will keep the sticky flies from landing on our food." Grandma folded her arms and proudly watched the flies land on the little tents.

Soon, my Aunt Londa, Uncle Randall, and cousin Kerry arrived to celebrate. Then, Mimi and Bompa carried over their aluminum lawn chairs. We spent the rest of the afternoon and evening eating, swinging on the swing set, lighting off the last of our snakes, firecrackers, and flowers, and playing with sparklers.

We watched the nighttime fireworks some place different every year. For a few years, we watched them in our own town of Livingston. One year, we drove to Atwater; another year, we drove to Merced. One year, we drove to the University in Turlock and lay on the grass to watch them light up right over our heads. That was also the year that we drove on the sidewalk to avoid getting stuck in the traffic, something that we still laugh about. One year we drove to Hilmar and sat in the football stands, and another year it poured down rain, so we didn't watch them at all. Every fireworks show was fun to watch, but some shows were more fun than others.

One of the most memorable of my childhood was the one that almost killed us. It was 1980 something, and Dad was busy dealing with pressing issues on the ranch. Mom didn't want us kids to miss out on the fireworks, so she drove us into Livingston for their big event. We got there early and parked in the dirt parking lot wedged between the high school football field and baseball diamond. She parked next to the fence so that we could be as close to the show as possible.

We'd gotten there so early the people in charge of the fireworks were still setting everything up. We stood by the fence and watched them for a while as more cars started to arrive, all filled with people. Gary, our good family friend, was right next to us. He took chairs out of his truck and set them up for him, Mom, and the other adults to sit in. Clint and I stood by the fence and talked to our friends. It wasn't yet dark, but the sun had set, and we were all filled with anticipation as the minutes ticked by.

Suddenly, the fireworks started to go off. Many adults looked at their watches and then up at the sky. A few even complained how silly it was for them to be lighting the fireworks off so early because we couldn't hardly see them. Everyone gathered closer to the fence to get a better view and watched in awe as they went off one after another. The next thing we knew, fireworks were shooting right at us, on the *ground!* Fireworks flew in all directions, and people were running everywhere.

Without hesitation, Gary grabbed us kids, threw us in the back of his small brown truck, and ordered us to lie down and close our eyes. He picked up a lawn chair and put it on top of us for more protection. It all happened so fast! Even though he told us to keep our eyes closed, I couldn't help but look around to see what was happening.

He used a lawn chair to shield himself. He directed my mom and the other adults who were close by to stand behind him. He was tall and towered over them. He moved quickly from side to side, dodging the flames that were headed right toward him and stomping out the sparks that landed close by.

There was fear in his eyes, but Gary seemed to think of everyone before he thought of himself. The feeling of extreme danger filled the air as fireworks continued to pop, hiss, and fly in all directions with loud bangs.

And then, as quickly as it had started, it was over. Everyone slowly emerged from their vehicles and other hiding places. Gary helped all of us kids climb out of his truck and checked each of us.

I don't remember anyone being hurt by the incident, but it's quite possible that Gary saved a few lives that day. Our family was forever thankful that he was there to protect us. It wasn't a fireworks show filled with pretty lights in the sky, but it was certainly a fireworks show that I'll never forget.

As the sky drew darker in 1984, and the last of the sparklers had been extinguished in a bucket of water, we all went to get in the blue ranch truck. Dad started it up, and Londa and Randall climbed into the passenger side. Kerry and our family piled in the bed of the truck. Mom sat up on the wheel well and held Cody tight as Clint, Kerry, and I settled in our spots on the tailgate, anticipating that it would bounce just enough to make us squeal as we drove along on the old dirt road.

"Remember not to hold onto the hinges!" Dad hollered out the window.

"Yeah, remember, don't hold onto the hinges of the tailgate," Mom reiterated. "You might get hurt."

I suddenly remembered the painful blood blister that I had once gotten from holding onto one of those too tightly as it bounced along. So, I scooted back a little further toward the bed of the truck to get better balance without having to hold onto anything.

"Everyone ready?" called Dad.

"*Ready!*" we all hollered.

The truck moved steadily from its parking spot and headed toward the rows and rows of grapevines. Dad drove along the dirt road and turned right toward the canal. He then drove on the road at the base of the canal until we reached a spot to park at the edge of my great-grandparents' ranch and Gallo's property. Dad, Londa, and Randall joined the rest of us in the bed of the truck while we all waited patiently for the fireworks to light up the sky.

"Oh, there's one!" Mom pointed to the west.

"There's another one!" Kerry pointed to the north.

Mom (Betty) and Dad (Gene) enjoying life. July 1984.

We spent the next hour oohing and aahing over the aerial fireworks of beautiful colors that lit up the sky in all directions. It was a spectacular sight! We were just a small group enjoying America's birthday together. Mom was happy that we weren't surrounded by a million people, and I was happy that I didn't have to plug my ears. Since the fireworks were so far away, we couldn't hear a sound. We laughed, visited, and enjoyed each other's company as another Fourth of July came to an end. It was so wonderful that I had completely forgotten all about my stubbed toe.

SWIMMING IN SUNSHINE

To learn how to swim, you must get in the water.

A s summer continued, the temperature reached well over a hundred degrees Fahrenheit, which was normal for summer in the Central Valley. July and August were sometimes so hot that we would joke about being able to fry an egg on the sidewalk. I'm sure it could have been done, but we never actually tried it.

We didn't have air conditioning in our house, so we spent as much time outside playing in the water as we could. We had a small blue plastic wading pool that all three of us kids could fit in if we squished close together. When we weren't splashing in that, we were running through the sprinkler, swimming in the canal, playing in the furrows during irrigation, or looking for tadpoles in the Merced River at Hagaman Park, just a short drive from our house.

Our favorite place to play in the water, though, was my grand-parents' front yards. Each of their houses had huge front lawns they would flood irrigate once or twice a month. They were special occasions that we never wanted to miss.

"I'm watering the lawn," Papa said one afternoon.

Clint and I hurried and got our bathing suits and shorts on. We each grabbed an inflatable swimming pool air mattress and ran over to Grandma and Papa's house as fast as our bare feet would take us.

"Ouch, ouch," we yelped as we ran through the hot sandy soil to find cool water. We hurried toward the back of their house to the valve that sat deep in the ground and watched patiently as the water bubbled out from the pipe. It slowly made its way around the corner and covered their entire yard with a foot or so of fresh, cool water.

Mom carried Cody over to join us, and Grandma had set up a few lawn chairs for her and Mom to sit on in the grass while they kept an eye on us.

Grandma walked through the cool water wearing her blue and white sundress. "It's so sultry out here, but…ooh, this is so cold."

"It's just right!" Clint belly flopped onto the grass with a splash.

Mom set Cody down on the water-covered grass.

"Cold!" he squealed.

We splashed water at each other then took turns running and sliding onto the pool of water. We fell into the giant puddle then pretended like we were swimming on the grass. We jumped on the air mattresses to see how far we could slide on them. After we were soaking wet, we ran back to the water valve to catch giant bullfrogs that were trapped inside the square area that surrounded the valve. We held the frogs and compared their sizes.

A puddle of yellow accumulated in my hand. "Yuck!"

"Haha, he peed on you!" Clint laughed loudly.

Papa walked over to us. "That's what happens when you hold them too long. Their bodies warm up, and they pee," he explained.

"Gross!" I dropped the frog into the water and washed my hands off with a quick splash.

We watched the big bullfrogs hop around until the water slowly disappeared into the rich soil beneath the luscious green lawn that had been thoroughly watered. It wouldn't need a good soaking again for a few more weeks.

Grandma gave each of us an Orange Sherbert Push-Up ice cream pop. We ate them as we slowly walked back to our house, dragging our air mattresses behind us.

When we got back to the house, Mom said, "Since we all have our bathing suits on, do you guys want to go and play in the canal?"

"Yes!" we both yelled immediately.

"Okay, finish your ice cream, then we'll walk down there. On our way we might see Dad working on the tractor."

When we finished, Mom got our orange arm floaties from the back porch for Cody and me. Then we each got a towel out of the bathroom cupboard and headed outside.

Clint and I got our air mattresses from the porch and dragged them behind us as we walked behind Mom and Cody on the hot sandy soil. We stopped often to find a shady spot beneath the grapevines to cool our feet, then we continued our walk to the canal. Finding shade was easy but finding shady spots without puncturevines or sandburs was a different challenge. Getting a sticker stuck in the bottom of our foot was much more painful than burning feet.

In the distance we saw Dad on the red tractor. We stopped to visit with him for a few minutes before continuing on our journey.

Finally, we reached our destination. Clint, Cody, and I stood at the base of the sandy canal bank, looking up at its steep sides as if it were Mount Everest. Mom quickly walked to the top. We scrambled to meet her, trying not to let our feet burn in the process. We stood at the top of the bank and looked down into the dirty water. We walked on the dirt to the far end of the canal, where we could see a muskrat swimming.

Mom blew air into the orange arm floaties and put them on Cody's and my arms, ensuring that they were secure. She walked on the cement bridge and carefully sat down on the edge, dangling her feet into the murky water. "Come over here. You can see the muskrat better."

We cautiously walked to meet her on the skinny cement bridge, then sat down next to her to dangle our feet in the cold water. The giant muskrat swam away and dove into the muddy water in the deepest part of the canal. We could no longer see him, but we knew he was there. The water in that part of the canal was about ten feet deep and closed off with wooden boards. It was the only area of the canal where sticks, garbage, and moss often accumulated. We closely watched the water for a few minutes, patiently waiting for him to pop his head back up. We soon got bored with trying to spot the muskrat and were anxious to go swimming.

"I'm tired of waiting. Let's get in the water," said Mom.

We pulled ourselves up from the bridge and followed her across the cement back to the sandy canal bank. Our wet feet sank, and we were soon covered in a mix of mud, wet dirt, and dust. We walked along the edge of the canal near the olive trees until we reached the swimming hole.

The two olive trees that stood near the canal bank were Bompa's pride and joy. He carefully picked the olives each fall and cured and brined them himself in old glass mayonnaise jars. Each November, the whole family dined on his delicious olives until our bellies hurt.

The swimming hole was the spot that was deemed safe enough for us to swim. It was the place right before the water flowed at rapid speed into the canal from another water source, and far enough from where the muskrats swam. The water in the swimming hole was about three feet deep all summer long.

We sat on the sand at the edge of the canal and slowly scooted down the angled cement embankment until we reached the cleanest water. Clint and I then floated around on our air mattresses.

Mom helped Cody into the water and held him close to her as she tried to teach him how to hold his breath underwater. We spent the afternoon splashing around and staying cool in the hot summer sun.

"Hungee," said Cody.

"I guess we should get back home," said Mom. "Here, you guys watch Cody while I go for a swim." She helped Cody scramble up to the top of the bank.

Clint and I took turns holding the white rope that dangled into the water and used it to help us climb out of the canal. Papa had attached the rope to a metal rod he had hammered into the dirt near the swimming hole. It made it easier for us to get out of the canal on our own.

Once all three of us were safe on the bank, Mom ducked underwater and disappeared. We watched patiently as she reemerged at the other end of the canal. She then swam back toward us and stood near the falls that flowed into the lower part of the canal, close to where we had been swimming. She took several more laps back and forth until she finally pulled herself up and out.

Our day of swimming in the canal had come to an end.

That wasn't the only place we swam during the hottest days of summer. We were blessed to have wonderful family friends who let us use their swimming pools whenever we wanted to. It just meant that we had to drive to their houses.

We went to Ben and Mary's when Clint was feeling well enough to play with their son, Chris, who was almost his same age.

"Kimmy, plug your nose and jump in!" Ben said as I stood on the ladder of their above-ground blue pool.

I plugged my nose and jumped into the cold water, then quickly bobbed up to get air. I could swim well underwater but was still trying to figure out the combination of jumping and swimming, as I still hadn't quite mastered swimming above water. Besides that, I had left my orange arm floaties at home and was feeling a little lost without them.

"That was a big splash!" Mary exclaimed with a chuckle in her voice.

Mom was looking at me. She must have noticed the panic in my eyes as I doggy paddled to the side. "It's just like swimming in Bill and Donna's pool," she said.

I had been swimming in Bill and Donna's pool many times in the past, but for some reason, the above ground pool just felt different to swim in. It felt bigger and deeper.

"It's the same?" I asked

"Yes, it's not any deeper than their pool. It just feels different because it's not buried in the ground."

I pondered that mystery as I put my head down and swam underwater to the other side of the pool to where Clint and Chris were standing. Swimming underwater was so much easier.

"It's much cleaner than swimming in the canal," said Ben.

Mom always reminded us how her dad threw her in the canal and said, "Swim!"

It was a story that I'd heard many times before, and frankly, it scared me. The sides of the canal were cement, and I imagined how bad it would hurt if she threw me too hard and I hit the side of the canal. Knowing, though, that would never actually happen because she had been a lifeguard and was trained to help people swim. Besides, when we swam in the canal by our house, she'd always make us climb in very carefully with both feet after she'd gotten in and checked for glass at the bottom of it. And regardless of where we were swimming, it was always safe and fun.

Our family had gone to Ben and Mary's house for an afternoon barbecue. They were foster parents and besides their son Chris, they had many other children stay with them that we'd gotten to know well over the years. It was always a happy home to visit.

After we had our fill of swimming, Mary asked, "Who's ready for a game of croquet?"

We got a towel from the edge of the pool and dried ourselves off. We then helped each other to put the wire wickets into the grass.

"Let's put some of them closer together," Chris suggested.

"Yeah," Clint said. "And let's put a few farther away so it will make it harder for everyone to get their ball through them."

"Yeah, let's do that." Chris agreed.

After all the wire wickets were in place, we each picked out a color ball and got a wooden mallet from the croquet stand that matched it. There were only six balls in the set and seven players, so I picked Mom to be on my team. We all spent the next hour playing. I have no idea who won the game that day, but I'm sure it was Clint; he always seemed to win at everything.

We spent the rest of the afternoon eating barbequed hot dogs and hamburgers, Mary's famous potato salad, and other scrumptious treats. Food had become kind of scarce at home during that time because paying for Clint's medicine took priority over groceries. We were getting free cheese and butter from the government, though, so most meals consisted of something made with cheese and butter. Grilled cheese sandwiches were a staple in our household. I actually loved grilled cheese, but a barbecued hamburger was a special treat, so I especially loved the food part of our visit to Ben and Mary's house.

Later that evening, when we were back home, Dad surprised us with a special movie night. He set up the portable screen in the living room along with the movie projector to play home movies that he and Mom had taken over the years with their 8mm movie camera. We got settled on the couch with a bowl of popcorn.

"Can we watch Woody Woodpecker first?" I asked.

"I want to watch Heckle and Jeckle first," said Clint.

"No, Woody Woodpecker is funnier!" I insisted.

"Wood." Cody piped in, probably not even knowing what he was talking about.

"We'll watch both of them," said Dad. "We'll watch Pepe Le Pew and the Pink Panther, too."

With that, it was settled, so we three kids relaxed and went back to eating popcorn while Mom turned off all the lights in the house to make it feel like a real movie theater. We all stared at the big white screen with enthusiasm and watched each movie that Dad played on the 8mm movie projector. Once all the professionally made movies were played, he put on the home movies.

There was no sound on the home movies, so all we could hear was our laughter and giggles as we watched younger versions of ourselves on the screen. After a few hours of movie watching, we were all ready for bed. Another summer day had come to an end.

Playing in the water at Grandma and Papa's house
when they flood irrigated their lawn.
Mom (Betty), Papa, Grandma and Clint. Summer 1982.

RUNNING AWAY

THE NEXT FEW DAYS were spent in Oakland, where once again, Clint was in the hospital. There was still talk of him dying and possibly needing a bone marrow transplant, but they were holding off on that for the time being. Some of the treatments seemed to be helping, and, in my opinion, Clint seemed "fine." I didn't notice anything different about him. He still had a lot of nose bleeds, was sleepy sometimes, and only ate certain foods, but he had just been swimming with me a few days before.

I had been sick one time with stomach flu, and that made me feel so awful that I couldn't even play with my toys, let alone want to go swimming. Clint still played with his toys and went swimming, so I thought he must not have been too sick. How could you die from an illness if you didn't act or feel really sick all the time? Maybe Clint was just special?

The older I got, the more I realized how much life just didn't make any sense at all. In the process of trying to figure it all out, I was starting to grow a bit jealous of all the attention that Clint was getting from being sick. People were even bringing him presents while he was in the hospital. He had just gotten a new Simon Says toy that talked and lit up red, yellow, blue, and green when you pressed on it. I wanted a Simon Says toy, too.

After spending several busy days at the hospital and staying a few nights at Rod and Donna's house in Concord, we were all back home again. Clint was feeling too awful to do anything but lie around and sleep, so I found myself wandering around the house trying to find something to do. Clint didn't even have enough energy to play with his new Simon Says toy. It didn't take long for the jealousy that I had felt before to quickly change to sadness. How terrible it was of me to be jealous of Clint being sick.

He must be so sad.

As the morning dragged on, I became bored. There was no school to go to, all my friends lived too far away to walk to their houses, and Cody was too little to play with me for very long.

"I'm bored," I told my mom.

"Bored? There's plenty to do. There's no reason to be bored."

"I can't find anything to do. This house is boring."

"I don't know how you can possibly say that."

I was feeling frustrated. "I'm going to run away from home and find somewhere else to live."

"Okay," she said. "You might want to pack a bag."

"I don't need a bag. I just need my big doll."

"How far do you think you'll get with just your big doll?"

"Far!" I said louder than I planned.

"Okay, I'll stand here and watch you out the window. You might want to get going before it gets too late."

I ran to my bedroom to grab my big doll, then swiftly walked out the front door that we hardly ever used. It was only used when the company came to visit. We regularly used the sliding glass door, but I was in a hurry, and the front door was closer to my bedroom than the sliding door was.

I quickly walked down the steps and down the sidewalk, I didn't go toward the Quonset or my grandparents' houses; I headed straight for the grapevines. I had no idea where I was going; I just knew that I wanted to get away from home. I turned around once to look and see if my mom was really watching me out the living room window. She was. I wanted to walk until she could no longer see me.

I made it to the first row of grapes, then the next. I turned and looked back at our house. It felt really far away. Maybe a little too far. Maybe I didn't want to run away from home after all. I didn't want to go home, though; I was bored there. I walked back to the first row of grapes and stopped to look around. I found a grapevine where the leaves were extra-large, and the vines were hanging all the way to the ground. It was the perfect place to hide. I crouched down on my knees and crawled under the cascading vines. I sat with my back leaning up against a wooden stake with my big doll in my lap. I looked up and saw bunches of baby grapes the size of peas. In a few months, they would be sweet and juicy enough to eat.

This is the perfect place to live.

I realized that as I sat in the cool shade of the large grape leaves that completely surrounded me.

Nobody will ever find me here. I can hide from the world.

I was filled with hope, sure that my mom could no longer see me from the living room window.

I set my big doll on the dirt and picked up a stick. I used it to draw pictures on the ground and make little trails that would be perfect to drive my little Hot Wheels cars on. I needed my cars!

Forgetting that I had *run away* from home, I hurried back to the house, the entire fifty yards, to get my Hot Wheels. I grabbed just a few then ran back to my *new house*.

I drove the little metal cars around for a little while before I decided that I needed other toys. Back and forth I went, several times to and from our house to my *new house* until I realized that I was getting hungry.

Food. I would eventually need to go home to eat. But I ran away from home. How could I go back? I sat there for a few minutes contemplating my decision when suddenly the grapevines moved like a set of curtains being drawn open.

Mom was holding a paper plate with half a peanut butter and jelly sandwich and barbequed potato chips on it. "I thought you might be hungry."

I was too nervous to speak. Mom had found me. Was she going to make me *move* back home?

"Do you want me to sit with you?"

That surprised me. "You want to sit in my house?"

"Of course! It's nice and cool in here." She motioned toward my big doll lying in the dirt.

"It is." I smiled up at her, realizing that she loved my *new home,* too.

We sat and talked while I ate my sandwich and chips. Once I was done, I asked her the question that I was dreading. "Do I have to go back home?"

"Nope. You can stay here in your little house as long as you want. Sometimes, we all need time alone," she said with a big smile on her face.

I beamed with joy as she took my paper plate from me and crawled out of my little house.

I peeked through my grapevine curtains and watched her walk back to our house. Once I saw that she was back inside, I went back to playing with my toys.

I continued playing in the dirt in my *new house* without a care in the world.

Mom said I could stay there as long as I wanted, but the truth was that I missed my brothers. I was ready to go home. I peeled back my grapevine curtains and ran to the house to find Mom in the kitchen.

"Mom, can I come home?"

"Are you ready to move back home?" I guess she wanted to make sure that I was sure of my decision.

"*Yes!*"

"Okay, let's go and get your toys."

She walked with me to my grapevine house and helped me carry all my toys back to the house. She told me how proud she was of me for not wandering too far from home. She also told me how I didn't have to *move* to my grapevine house, but that I could think of it as more of a playhouse that I could go and play in any time that I wanted during the summer.

Once fall arrived, the grapevines would no longer hang to the ground like curtains. They would be trimmed and wrapped on the vines to prepare for new growth in the spring. Summer was the perfect time to escape from the world, though, and I now had a place to do that. Running away from home that day taught me that sometimes it's okay to hide from the world for a little while. It also taught me that I was still loved even at times when I was all alone.

HARVEST TIME

Hard work and good soil made for full bellies.

A NEW SCHOOL YEAR had begun, and harvest was in full swing. The aroma of crushed leaves could be smelled for miles. The big yellow grape harvester sat behind our house as Dad hosed off every inch of it to ensure it was thoroughly clean for harvesting later that night. It stood so tall that when I climbed up on top of it, I imagined that I was on the Eiffel Tower. Its beater bars worked hard each night, beating the grapes off the vines and onto the black conveyor belts. As Papa carefully drove it over each row of grapes, workers walked behind the harvester, watching for any vines, wood, or wire that might get tangled up in the giant machine.

Dad, neighbors, friends, and other workers would take turns driving the tractors pulling grape gondolas. The tractors would have to be driven at a crawl in the row next to the harvester to catch the grapes that rolled off the long, outstretched metal conveyor belt arm. Two workers had to sit on top of the harvester to catch any leaves, sticks, or critters that might have been shaken off the vines and onto the belts; only grapes were to be dumped into the harvester.

Dad finished spraying off the giant machine.

"Can I help with harvest tonight?" I asked.

"I don't see why not. It's Friday, so you don't have school tomorrow."

I beamed with excitement knowing that as soon as the sun went down, the harvester would be starting up. Papa said he liked to harvest at night because the sugar content of the grapes was higher. The wine makers liked the sugar content to be at a certain level to make the best-tasting wine. I know that the adults didn't like having to work at night, but I thought it was amazing to stand high up on the harvester and be closer to the stars as they twinkled in the sky.

We ate a quick dinner that night, and Mom packed sandwiches, chips, and snacks in small brown paper bags for her and Dad. They would be eating them later sometime during the night as they both helped with harvest. I was watching *Emergency* on TV when Grandma showed up at our house a little after sunset to stay with Clint, Cody, and me.

"I thought that I could help with the harvest tonight?" I asked Grandma impatiently as Mom and Dad left to go down to the field.

"One of them will come and get you during their break," said Grandma.

My brothers and I made blanket forts and played with toys while Grandma sat in the gold chair patiently watching over us.

Before I knew it, Dad walked into the house. "Who wants to ride on the harvester?"

"Not me." Grandma chuckled.

All three of us kids shouted, "Me!"

"Okay, come with me." Dad motioned toward the door.

He carried Cody, and we followed him outside. Somehow, we all managed to find a spot to sit on the little red tractor as Dad drove us to where the harvester was parked. The closer we got to the harvester, the stronger the smell of grapes and crushed leaves became.

We climbed down from the tractor and walked to the giant yellow machine. Mom was patiently waiting for us by the ladder. She helped each of us climb up to the top of the harvester.

Once at the top, we were greeted by Papa, who was standing next to the big steering wheel.

He grinned. "Who's ready to work?"

"I want to drive!" said Clint

"Okay, you show me how to do it," Papa said.

Clint sat down on the seat and pretended to steer the big black wheel like a captain of a ship.

Mom carried Cody to where she was working on the conveyor belt. She showed him how she pulled sticks off and threw them into the sea of grapevines on the ground. She sat down next to the conveyor belt with Cody held tightly in her arms.

Papa put earmuffs on each of us kids to protect our ears from the loud rumbling of the harvester. He put the harvester into gear and revved up the engine, then he helped Clint steer the giant machine down the row.

Dad drove the tractor in the next row as grapes carefully fell into the gondola being pulled behind him.

I helped Mom throw as many sticks and leaves off the belt as I could before the harvester came to a stop at the end of the row.

Papa grabbed his metal lunch box from beside the steering wheel. "It's break time!"

He handed each of us a snack, a Ding Dong wrapped in aluminum foil.

We carefully unwrapped the chocolate cake treat, and we all took a big bite. We were surprised to find that there was a cream filling hiding in the middle of the little round cakes.

Papa smiled. "Good, huh?"

Clint and I slowly ate the rest of our special treat. "Mm-hmm," we both mumbled.

Cody was too busy eating it to say anything.

After we finished our tasty snack, we said our goodbyes to Papa. Mom helped each of us kids down from the harvester.

Dad met us at the bottom of the ladder and gave us hugs.

Mom used a flashlight to guide our way back to the house. We weren't too far away, so it didn't take long to get home. Once there, Mom stayed, got us cleaned up, and ready for bed.

 Dad picked her up about half an hour later.

Once the gondola was filled with grapes, he dumped them into the big black trailer. The grapes would sometimes sit there for a day or two, so the smell of sour grapes filled the air for weeks on end. After they were dumped in the trailer, he and Mom went back to the field to finish working for the night.

Grandma sat in the living room watching TV for a while. She usually left once we were settled and asleep.

Many nights of harvest over the years that followed, Grandma would bring a box of Cracker Jacks to each of us kids when she'd check on us while Mom and Dad were working down the field.

She'd help us dig through the box to find our Cracker Jack prize hiding inside. They were something fun, like stickers, tattoos, or little plastic magnifying glasses. But Grandma would complain about how the prizes weren't nearly as good as they used to be. The treat was delicious, but I would usually just eat the peanuts and let Grandma, Clint, and Cody share my caramelized popcorn.

Everything on the ranch, and nearby ranches, had to be harvested, not just the grapes. We helped the neighbors rake up almonds, and in turn, they helped us shake the walnuts from our giant trees that lined the end of the grape rows.

There were two different varieties of walnuts; Black and English walnuts. The Black ones had a soft green exterior that turned black as they ripened. They are very messy and not easy to crack open.

We put the English walnuts in large wooden boxes, and the Black walnuts were put in large burlap sacks. Then they were all sent off to Blue Diamond for processing. The English walnuts were my favorite; they were perfect for cracking open and eating once they were ripe.

It was an early Saturday morning in the fall when Mom urged us to put on our jackets and shoes. "It's time to go and help with the walnuts." She zipped up Cody's coat and ushered all of us kids outside.

I had forgotten where the walnut trees were and that they had to be raked up every fall. "Where are we going?"

"Down the field. Your Dad and Papa are already down there working."

We walked to the end of the road closest to our house. Instead of turning right toward the canal, we turned left. As we got closer, we could see one of the English walnut trees moving wildly.

I pointed in the direction of the seventy plus year old walnut tree shaking violently in the close distance. "What's happening to that tree?"

"Our neighbor CV is using the tree shaker to help get all the walnuts off. Just like he does with his almond trees," Mom explained.

"Oh, I want to watch!" I started to run toward the tree. "Come on, Cody, run with me!" I didn't ask Clint because he wasn't feeling well enough.

Cody's little legs moved as fast as they could as we ran. When we got near the tree, we stood far enough away to not get hit by flying walnuts but were close enough to watch the yellow tree shaker. It clamped onto the trunk of the giant walnut tree and forcibly shook it back and forth. The large yellowing leaves fluttered as hundreds of walnuts dropped to the ground with each intense shake. Mom and Clint reached Cody and me just in time to watch the last shake of the tree.

When it stopped, CV backed up the shaker and drove to the next walnut tree.

Mom scooted us along toward the work truck. "Let's get busy." She lifted rakes out of the back of the truck and handed one to each of us.

Dad held up his big metal rake. "It's a good thing that you're all here to help us!"

Mom, Clint, and I used the wooden handled, green plastic rakes to scrape up as many walnuts as we could. We coughed at the dust that flew everywhere as we dragged our rakes across the dirt. The walnuts sounded like marbles dropping on a hardwood floor. We diligently raked them into piles, then Dad and Papa shoveled the piles of walnuts into large wooden boxes. Later they would be picked up by trucks and delivered to Blue Diamond for packing and selling.

After every last walnut from that tree had been put in the boxes, Papa announced that it was time for a short break. We drank water out of little Dixie cups that we filled up with the big, water cooler in the back of the truck.

Papa pulled a nutcracker from his back pocket. We watched him crack a walnut. "Want a bite?" Papa handed me a piece of walnut.

"Mmm…" The rich, nutty taste filled my mouth with a soft crunch.

Mom smashed one open with a rock. "The best part of raking up walnuts is eating them."

We spent the next few minutes sitting on the ground, drinking water, and eating walnuts. I had just enough time to finish eating two whole walnuts before it was time to get back to work.

We piled into the back of the truck, and Papa drove to the next walnut tree. I don't know exactly how many walnut trees we raked, but it was enough to keep us busy for most of the day.

The Black walnuts would be harvested a few weeks later. That was a job nobody wanted to do because they were a lot messier. We used rakes, shovels, and our hands to ensure that every walnut was put in the giant burlap gunny sacks before they were sent off to Blue Diamond. The smell of greasy burlap would permeate into the skin of our black stained hands that the residue left behind, and no matter how hard we scrubbed, it would take days before it all washed away. Nobody looked forward to that harvesting job.

As soon as we got back home after a busy day of raking up walnuts, Clint and I treated ourselves to a fresh pomegranate off Grandma and Papa's tree. We stood in the shade of the giant tree, looking up at its outstretched branches as the large fruit hung down like giant red glass ornaments on a Christmas tree.

"We have to find ones that are a little cracked open, and that aren't too covered with ants," said Clint.

"Why do they have to be cracked?"

"Because that's how we know that they're ripe."

"Oh, I think I found one!" I pointed way too high for either of us to reach.

Clint walked around the tree. "Let's try to find one that I can reach."

After several minutes of walking under every branch of the tree, we finally found ones that were perfect for each of us. Clint twisted two of them until they finally released their grip from the tree. He kept one for himself and planned to give the other one to Mom.

I watched how Clint freed the pomegranates from the tree's grasp and copied his action and picked my own perfectly cracked open fruit. As we walked back to the house, I blew off a few black ants that were scurrying to hide inside the crack on the large red fruit. We walked through our door and headed toward the kitchen when Mom quickly shooed us outside.

Clint handed Mom one of the pomegranates. "I have one for you, Mom."

She followed us as we stepped out onto the porch. "Why do we have to stay outside?"

"Because pomegranates stain. You need to eat them outside so that you don't get the juice on anything in the house," Mom explained. "You guys go ahead and eat yours, I'll eat mine later."

It wasn't until much later in life that I learned just how badly pomegranates stain things. I spent one whole weekend in my twenties making grenadine and jelly with the juice from the pomegranates that I picked from my grandparents' luscious tree. Every white cabinet in our kitchen was covered in red splatters as I squeezed juice from the seeds. I spent hours making the scrumptious treats and even more time cleaning up the mess that I had made. It was in my cleaning frenzy when I remembered my mom explaining to me the reason why we needed to eat our pomegranate seeds outside when we were kids.

"Let's sit over here." Clint led me to the stairs at the end of our porch that faced the grape vineyard to the south of our house.

We sat on the steps and picked the seeds out of our giant pomegranates one by one. The sweet red juice popped from each little seed as we placed them in our mouths.

Clint and I talked about everything from the weather to his doctors as we ate the delectable treat. When we couldn't stand to eat anymore and were covered from head to toe in pomegranate juice, we took what was left and ran over to the tree that stood tall near the Quonset hut. We threw the remains near the trunk of the tree in hopes that the ants would enjoy what was left of our treat. We ran back home, knowing that our day of being outside had come to an end as baths would soon be in order.

The busy weekend of harvest chores continued into Sunday. After morning breakfast, services at the Baptist church in town, and a quick lunch back at home, it was time to help pick persimmons.

It wasn't until I was much older that I learned about there being several different varieties of persimmons; I just thought they were all exactly like the ones on the ranch. I don't know exactly which variety my grandparents had in their front yard; I only know that they weren't the kind that could be eaten right off the tree.

Grandma told us, "They'll make your mouth pucker." They were the type of persimmon that was best used in baking things like bread and cookies. My grandparents' were bright orange and pointy at one end. Just enough that little black paper witch hats rested perfectly on them when we'd decorate them for Halloween.

Grandma handed me a small stack of paper sacks. "Here, Kimmy, you carry these over to your dad."

I walked over to where he and Papa were looking up at the persimmon tree in Grandma and Papa's backyard. I set the paper sacks on the grass, careful not to step on any fruit that was squishy and oozing with rot.

"Let's start with this tree." Papa held a long stick in his hand with an orange basket-looking thing at one end. He reached up as far as he could and hooked one of the persimmons in its grasp. He pulled the stick toward his chest, and the fruit fell into the basket. Dad opened one of the paper sacks, and Papa placed it into the bag. They did the same thing over and over until the sacks were full.

As Papa worked at getting all the persimmons he could reach with his stick, Dad and I picked the ones within our reach. Clint usually helped, but he wasn't feeling up to it that day. I continued to pick the orange persimmons that I could reach while he set up the ladder to reach the ripe fruit. After we finished one tree, we moved on to the next.

In my grandparents' front yard there were three trees in total that were loaded to the gills with persimmons. That day we filled enough sacks to feed a small army. Once we finished, we loaded the fruit into the bed of our truck, and Dad drove it all into town. I rode along with him to Serv-All in Livingston to deliver the freshly picked fruit.

Frankie, a good friend of ours, was the store manager. He greeted us once we got there and helped us carry the persimmons into the store. We put the bags on the ground in the back storage area. Then one by one Dad and I transferred them from the sacks to boxes that were lined with purple paper mats. They had rounded areas perfect for each persimmon to fit in, and they could look nice on the shelf in the fresh produce department.

After Frankie carefully inspected and counted each persimmon, Dad and I put the fresh fruit in the boxes. After they were all transferred, Frankie paid my dad a quarter a piece for each of them.

Even though they were technically my grandparents' persimmons, Papa let my parents keep the money for all the ones that were sold to the store. It was their way of contributing to Clint's medical bills that had accumulated to well over a million dollars.

(That would be equivalent to well over three million dollars in 2026, when this book was published.)

Farming certainly wasn't a rich with money kind of life. It could be considered more of a calling, because in general, farm life was pretty stressful, and harvest time always compounded those stresses.

That, in conjunction with a son who was dying of cancer and insurmountable medical bills, it's a wonder how my parents ever slept at night. I was too young to understand the weight of it all, but it was never hidden from me. The stresses were life lessons that helped us all to cope with whatever was placed before us.

Harvest may have been a stressful time of year, but it was also a special season that involved a lot of quality time with family and extraordinary treats.

Harvest taught me independence, expecting the unexpected, and preparing for possible setbacks, but most of all, it taught me that we were *very loved*.

Papa and Dad (Gene) preparing the grape harvester for harvest.

HALLOWEEN

~KIMBERLEY'S THOUGHT~

CLINT WAS BACK in the hospital again. So that I didn't miss any days of school, I spent a night with my cousin Kerry at her house in Delhi, then at my grandparents' house on the ranch, then one at Bill and Donna's. Those days I was reminded many times how important school was and shouldn't be missed, unless it was absolutely necessary. Some might say that I had been shuffled from place to place, but I didn't see it that way at all. Each day was a new adventure and a chance to visit with those whom I loved to spend time with. I did often worry, though, that I'd miss something important that took place at the hospital. I always wondered if Clint was having fun with his puppet, Coco, and if his doctors had healed him of his cancer yet.

After several days of staying with family and friends, it was finally time when I was going to be able to stay a whole night at home in my own bed. I climbed off the bus that stopped right in front of my grandparents' house and ran straight home. My brother was finally back, and I couldn't wait to see him. I opened the sliding door, skirted around the pool table, and stopped at the breakfast bar. Still wearing his pajamas, Clint was sitting on a barstool. We were never allowed to wear our pajamas during the day unless we were really sick, so I gathered quickly that Clint must have been feeling horrible.

"Hi, Kimmy," he said, without even trying to attack me.

Oh man, he must really be sick.

"Are you sick?" Of course, I knew he was dying of cancer, but I thought he must be sick with something else besides *just* the cancer to still be in his pajamas.

"Yeah, I feel pretty crummy. But I'll be okay. I'm fine. I just didn't feel like getting dressed today."

"Oh, okay." But I wasn't convinced that he was actually fine. His "fine" reminded me of my daily encounter at school with the lunch card lady. Even though I was a big first grader, she still asked me how my brother was every time I saw her. Not wanting to have to explain anything, I continued to stick with my safe answer of, "Fine." It was just easier that way.

Interrupting my thoughts, Mom's voice boomed from her bedroom. "Hi! How was school?"

"It was fun."

Mom walked into the kitchen. "We're going to make witches."

"How?"

"With the persimmons." She gestured to the bowl full on the kitchen counter.

"For Halloween?" It must be getting close.

"Yep! Your dad is busy on a fire call, so this will give us something to do until he gets home."

I was excited. "Aw, they're going to be so cute!"

"So *cute*," Clint mocked me. Maybe he was feeling better than he knew.

We spent the next hour cutting and gluing pieces of construction paper to create the perfect little orange witches. We turned the persimmons upside down, so the green stem became the witch's necklace. The pointed end of the persimmon was where we put the black pointed hat that we created by rolling the paper just right. We cut purple, green, and black construction paper into long strips and glued them on each persimmon to create the long hair on each little witch. Mom used her scissors on some of them to carefully curl the ends of the construction paper so that some of the witches had curls at the end of their hair. We then cut out eyes, noses, and mouths. They varied in color but also looked similar. We would carve pumpkins in the coming days, but for now, the little persimmon witches filled the house with joy.

As we worked, Mom asked Clint and me, "What do you two want to dress up as for Halloween this year?"

Clint announced immediately, "I want to be a vampire!"

I shrugged. "I don't want to be anything. Costumes are scary."

"Costumes don't have to be scary. You can be anything you want to be," said Mom.

Clint's eyebrows shot up. "You could be a witch."

"No. That's scary!" The thought made me shiver.

Clint laughed. I know he knew I'd be too scared to dress up as a witch.

"But you could be a cute one, like these." Mom held one of the persimmon witches in her hand.

I didn't say anything.

She smiled. "Don't worry, you have lots of time to think about it." Mom put the finishing touches on a few of the witches.

"You're going to want to dress up as something, though," Clint said. "Or else you can't go trick-or-treating with me." He paused for a second then he added, "So, no candy."

Hmm. He had a point. I needed to think of something.

Just then, we heard the tractor behind our house. We looked out the kitchen window and saw Papa drive by.

"See?" That meant Cody wanted to be picked up so he could see out the window.

Mom lifted him, and Cody pointed to Papa.

Cody always loved seeing Papa and had a special knack for making our grandpa smile and laugh at any given moment. In fact, he had a knack for making all of us do the same, no matter the circumstance.

We all walked out on the back porch to wave to Papa.

Cody shouted, "Pop Pop."

We all laughed as Cody continued to repeat the phrase, "Pop pop" over and over again. He may have just been referring to the popping sound that the tractor was making, but from that day on, our grandpa Jerry was known to us as Papa. A name that stuck for the remainder of his life.

A few days later, our family piled into our car and drove behind our house to a neighbor's field that was full of pumpkins. We'd been given permission for each of us to pick one to carve into a jack-o-lantern.

Clint found his pumpkin right away. I was sure that it was the largest, fattest pumpkin in the whole patch. I watched him proudly carry it to the car, then he sat there and watched the rest of us walk through the field trying to find our perfect pumpkins.

Mom helped Cody find one that he was able to carry on his own, and Dad helped me try to decide on one that I insisted needed to be "cute." After a long time, I finally settled on one that was flat and round. It was shaped more like a fat pancake than a pumpkin, but Dad convinced me that I could make it cute when I carved it.

The cold, gloomy, cloudy days of autumn brought us closer to Halloween night, and I still hadn't thought of what to dress up as so I could go trick-or-treating with my brothers.

One day after school, I was at Grandma and Papa's house helping Grandma work on her puzzle. Suddenly, someone walked into their house through the back door. Whoever it was wore a black cape and gloves. We couldn't see the person's face because their cape was covering it, but they were about the same height as my grandparents, so I knew it was an adult.

The person came closer to us and looked right at me. Their face was clear and melted-looking.

I screamed!

It was creepy! I ran and hid behind Papa's legs; he and Grandma started to laugh.

What was so funny? Nothing about that creepy person was funny! Then, the person lifted what I realized was a mask. It was *Mom*. She was laughing so hard that she couldn't even talk.

"Why did you scare me like that?" I was almost in tears.

She still laughed. "Because I wanted to see how you'd react. Now I know."

I was so mad at her for trying to scare me, and even more because she thought scaring me was funny. Later in the day, she scared both of my brothers with the same creepy outfit. Clint thought it was funny, but Cody had the same reaction that I did. He was so scared of Mom's mask that he wouldn't even let her hold him when we went trick-or-treating on Halloween night. He stayed close to my dad's side.

Mom loved Halloween and all the creepiness that went with it. I could never understand why she loved scary things so much. I was really hoping that she could help me decide on a costume that wouldn't scare me so that I could go trick-or-treating.

Mom said, "I came to get you because we're going to carve our pumpkins. Mom and Dad, you can join us if you want."

Before long, we were sitting on our newspaper-lined kitchen floor scooping out the "guts" of our pumpkins with our bare hands.

"Eww sticky!" Cody kept repeating as he tried to get the gooey orange pulp off his hands.

Clint and I pulled out all the seeds and stringy pumpkin threads that we could.

Grandma and Papa chuckled as Dad tried to clean Cody's hands off with a wet paper towel.

We spent the rest of the evening using black permanent marker to draw the places that we wanted to cut out on our pumpkins. Mom, Dad, Grandma, and Papa helped us cut out each shape until our pumpkins looked like the jack-o-lanterns that we had conjured up in our minds.

Dad was right, I was able to make my pumpkin look cute with a big toothless smile.

Clint's was fierce looking with pointed teeth, and Cody's had a round mouth with matching round eyes. All in all, our little pumpkin family blended in well with our persimmon witches that were now sitting on the pool table.

"You guys need to wash up and get ready for bed," Mom said as Dad cleaned up the pumpkin mess from the kitchen floor.

Grandma reminded us, "That's right, Halloween is tomorrow."

My eyes widened. "Tomorrow?"

Papa laughed. "Yep, and you're going to get lots of candy."

I went to clean up, and my mind became consumed with ideas of costumes, witches, goblins, and scary things.

Clint and I were getting ready for bed. "Can I sleep with you tonight?"

He laughed. "Why, are you scared a ghost is going to get you?"

"Yes!" I answered louder than I thought possible.

He smiled at me. "Sure. I'll keep you safe."

With that, I relaxed a little as I quickly put on my pajamas and climbed up the ladder to his bed before he changed his mind. We talked for a long time about costumes, candy, and things that were less scary. I still had no idea what I was going to be for Halloween, but somehow, I knew it would all work out.

Clint and I eventually drifted off to sleep.

It was Halloween morning, and Clint was feeling well enough to go to school. He hurried out of bed, put on his black pants and cape, then had Mom paint his face white to help him look like a vampire.

I watched Mom cover his face in white. I thought it looked like fun, so I decided that I wanted to do that, too.

"Can you paint *my* face, Mom?"

"We don't have enough paint for your whole face, but I can put makeup on you. Eyeliner, blush, and eyeshadow," said Mom.

"Okay, what can I dress up as so that I can wear makeup?"

"I'm not sure. Maybe a gypsy?"

"What's a gypsy?"

"Someone who likes to travel. Gypsies don't live in one spot. They move around a lot and like to dance and play instruments. Some of them wear a lot of makeup."

"Okay, that doesn't sound scary. I'll be a gypsy."

It was finally settled. Though I didn't really know what it was, I was going to be a gypsy for Halloween. At school that day, I had my biggest smile when I walked in the parade wearing a dress, a brown wig, and lots of make-up.

Later that night, Mom redid my face before we went trick-or-treating. After my makeup was complete, she redid Clint's vampire paint, complete with fake red blood oozing from his plastic fangs.

Then, Mom helped Cody dress up in a handmade little devil costume. He wore red sweats, a hand-sewn red cape, and a pitch-fork made with a red wooden handle, complete with aluminum foil tines. Once all our costumes were complete, Mom again put on her black cape and creepy mask that scared me too much to even look at her.

Mom ushered us into the family room. "Let's get a picture."

Clint and I stood at the end of the pool table while Mom set

Cody on the top, and Dad took the picture of us in our costumes.

"Where's your costume, Dad?" I asked.

"I'm wearing it. Can't you see it?" He made a goofy face, sticking his tongue out sideways and laughing.

I giggled. "You're silly."

Before driving to town, we walked to Grandma and Papa's house carrying our pillow cases. We used to go trick-or-treating carrying brown paper sacks. Then one year, when I was really little, and my bag became too heavy for me to carry. I started dragging it across the damp lawns. It got a hole in it, and Mom and Dad trailed behind me picking up the candy that was falling out.

Ever since then, Mom decided that we should use pillow cases to collect our candy in place of paper sacks.

Once we got to Grandma and Papa's house, instead of knocking like real trick-or-treaters, we walked right in and hollered "Trick-or-treat!"

"Oh! You scared us!" Grandma pretended. She put her hands on her chest.

Grandma said to Mom, "You really do look creepy, Betty." She scrunched up her nose and laughed.

"I think Pauline has something special for you," said Papa. "We don't get many trick-or-treaters out here."

"I do, just a minute." Grandma disappeared into her bedroom, then came back out holding something behind her back.

"Open up your pillow cases," she said.

"Trick-or-treat," Clint and I said, and Cody mimicked us.

Grandma put a full-size Hershey's candy bar in each of our pillow cases.

Our eyes opened wide when we looked at the special treat. It was going to be a fun night!

"You'd better go to Mimi and Bomp's. I think they might have something for you, too," said Papa.

We thanked Grandma and Papa and left.

We walked across their yard in the dark and made our way to the cement patio that led us to Mimi and Bompa's front door. Thankfully, their porch light helped to guide our way through the dark green ivy that lined the roof of their patio.

Mom opened their front door as the rest of us trailed closely behind her.

"Trick-or-treat!" Clint and I announced.

We walked in, and I could see Mimi sitting on the couch by the fireplace.

Bompa was in the kitchen. "Well, what do we have here?"

Mimi laughed. "Ohh, you all look so…different. Do we have something for these trick-or-treaters, Maynard?"

"Hmmm, I think I can find something."

We opened our pillow cases as Bompa pretended to put an apple and an orange into them and then he laughed. He put the fruit on the table and magically replaced it with full-size Baby Ruth candy bars.

We couldn't believe our eyes! We already had more candy in our bags than we had seen since Easter.

"Thank you!" we said and quickly made our way toward the door.

"You're welcome. Have fun tonight in those costumes," called Bompa.

"And be careful," added Mimi.

"We will. Thank you!" said Mom.

She did sound just like Mom, regardless of the creepy disguise that made her look much different.

We quickly hurried across the dirt to meet Dad, who was waiting for us in the car. We were off to town to go trick-or-treating, and I could hardly wait.

Once we got to town, Dad parked the car at the end of a street that was lined with houses. Other families were already walking on the sidewalks with bags full of candy. We all piled out of the car, and Clint and I knocked on the door of the first house that we came to.

"Trick-or-treat!" we called and opened our big white pillow cases. Little bits of candy were dropped inside. It was just the first house, and we were already thrilled to have so much candy in our bags. Clint and I ran to the next house as Mom, Dad, and Cody trailed behind us.

"Don't get too far ahead of us," called Dad.

"We won't," Clint assured him, then encouraged me to keep up with him.

"We have to hurry and get to the houses where the lights are dimmer than the others because that means they're almost out of candy," Clint explained to me.

"Really?"

"Yeah, if the lights are really bright, that means they have a lot of candy left. If the lights are dim, that means that they're almost out of candy, and if there's no porch light on, that means no candy. So, we have to hurry before all of the porch lights are out."

"Okay." I believed every word that my big brother was telling me.

The rest of the night was a full-on race to see who could get to the houses first. Surprisingly, Cody did a really good job of keeping close behind us. And, somehow, he ended up with more candy than we did.

As soon as we got home, we sat on the living room floor and dumped out our big white pillow cases. Heaping piles of candy sat in front of each of us. We couldn't believe our eyes. It was more candy than we had ever seen in our entire lives.

Clint held up a pink sucker. "Do you want to trade?"

"We're supposed to inspect it all first." Mom took off her creepy, melted face looking mask so that we could hear her clearly.

"For what?" I asked.

"For razor blades and stuff. At least that's what they said on the news."

"Razor blades?" Clint and I shrieked at the same time.

Mom said calmly, "Just look and make sure that none of your candy looks like it has been tampered with."

"Tampered?"

"Make sure that none of it looks like it's been opened."

"Or eaten." Dad laughed as he grabbed a fun-size Krackel candy bar out of Cody's pile and ate it.

We all laughed, and Cody didn't seem to care.

Halloween 1983. Mom (Betty) wearing her creepy mask,
I'm dressed up as a gypsy, Clint pretending to
be a vampire, and Cody dressed as a little devil.

Clint and I counted, sorted, and traded candy as Cody fell asleep right in his own pile of Halloween sweets. Once Clint and I had handled all the candy exchanges, Mom and Dad let us eat one piece of candy each before they gathered it in separate bowls and put them in the kitchen.

We were reminded that we had school the next morning, so it was time to wash all the Halloween makeup off our faces, brush our teeth, and get to bed.

Reluctantly, we did as we were told.

The night that we'd been planning for weeks ahead of time had come to an end, and it turned out to be a lot more fun than I had ever anticipated. I had prepared myself to be scared that night, but the only costume that scared me was my mom's. She loved that mask and wore it several Halloweens in a row after that. I never grew to fully embrace the love for Halloween like she did, but I did enjoy the time that I spent with my family. Even times of fear, anxiousness, and the unexpected can capture some of the very best memories.

MAKE-A-WISH

*Enjoy that things are happening
instead of crying because they are ending.*

~KIMBERLEY'S THOUGHT~

AFTER HALLOWEEN had come and gone, life continued on as normal, with each day bringing the unexpected. Living so far out in the country made it abnormal for us to have company at our house, and in the midst of the unexpected, we were preparing for just that.

My parents' friends, Ben and Mary, Bill, Gary, and Leon, would stop by and say "Hi" quite often, but I didn't consider them company. They were friends. We'd have parties at our house a few times a year, but only friends and family came to those, not company. I always thought of "company" as people that I'd never met before, or people that weren't yet our friends. So, when Mom and Dad explained that we needed to clean the house to prepare for company, it was as if the President was coming to visit.

We spent one whole Saturday cleaning every inch of the house. Laundry, vacuuming, mopping, dusting, knocking down spider webs, putting toys away, scrubbing toilets, and even putting our "good towels" out on the towel rack for company to dry their hands with. Finally, after the whole house looked as if it were brand new, we all sat down together to eat dinner.

"Who's coming over?" I asked curiously, still wondering why we had gone to so much work to clean the house so nicely.

"Some people from the Make-A-Wish Foundation are coming to talk to Clint," said Dad.

"What is Make-A-Wish?"

"It's an organization that helps to grant the wishes of children who are critically ill. They help to make a dream come true for kids who aren't expected to live very long," Mom explained.

"Oh. Clint, what are you going to wish for?" I asked excitedly, not fully understanding the heaviness of the conversation.

"I think I'm going to ask for a three-wheeler, but I have some other things in mind if they aren't able to get that."

"Yeah, we're not sure if that's the kind of thing that they'll give as a wish or not. Most wishes that they grant to kids are things like being a cop for a day, trips to Disneyland, or to a baseball game. Things like that," Mom explained.

The Make-A-Wish Foundation is a non-profit organization that began in 1980 with the granting of one wish to a critically ill boy or girl. The organization now has tens of thousands of volunteers, donors, and supporters who work diligently to grant the wishes of every child with a critical illness. Many believe that granting a child's wish can be the spark that helps them to see light in the darkness, that gives them the courage and strength to fight harder against their illness. Since that first wish was granted in 1980, research has shown that a child's wish being carried out was a turning point in their treatment, not just for the child but for the whole family. The relief of traumatic stress, even if for a day, can have impacts that last a lifetime. Our family is a testament to that.

Finally, our company had arrived to not only talk with Clint, but with all of us. A very nice man and woman from the Make-A-Wish Foundation came in with briefcases and clipboards in hand. They looked more like news reporters than wish-granters, but they were cheerful and compassionate. They introduced themselves and spoke to each of us individually in hopes of gaining knowledge of the situation that we were dealing with. They genuinely wanted to understand how each of us felt about leukemia, the cancer that was wreaking havoc on my brother's body. They then spent the remainder of their time talking to Clint about what his wish was. After they seemed to have gathered all the information they were seeking, they left with warm hugs and goodbyes.

"Did they grant you your wish?" I asked Clint after the Make-A-Wish people had driven away.

"Not yet, but they said they are going to try," he said cheerfully.

"Did you ask for the three-wheeler?"

"I did. They don't know if they can get me one, but they said they're going to do their best. I really think it's going to happen, though. I asked them to bring you and Cody something, too."

"You did? Why?"

"Because you and Cody deserve a wish, too. You're the ones who give me the strength to keep going on the days when I think I can't fight anymore. We are a family. Me being sick is hard for all of us, so we all deserve to be happy for a day."

I hugged him. "Ohhhh, that's so sweet."

The Make-A-Wish foundation moved quickly, and within just a few days, the nice man and woman were back at our house again, but this time they were accompanied by actual news reporters. We were going to be on TV!

"We're going to be on TV?" Mom adjusted the hot rollers in my hair.

"Yes. Isn't that exciting? That's why I asked you to put on your very best outfit. The whole world is going to see you!"

My mind wandered as Mom took the hot rollers out of my hair and put a little plastic hairclip in my bangs to help keep them out of my eyes. It was the prettiest I'd ever seen my hair. I grinned as I looked at myself in the bathroom mirror.

I was going to be on TV! The thought excited me so much that I had completely forgotten about the reason why any of it was even happening.

"They're ready for us!" Clint called into the bathroom where Mom and I were finishing getting ready.

"Hurry!" He added excitedly.

Mom and I quickly put on our jackets and followed him outside. It was a cold morning, and thick overcast covered the sky like a heavy white blanket. A big white van that had the word "NEWS" printed on the side of it was parked in front of my grandparents' house. Grandma and Papa were outside talking with the Make-A-Wish people as the news crew set up their camera. Dad was already busy talking to all of them, holding Cody in his arms.

"Everyone's here! We're ready to roll," someone said.

Just then, the news reporter had all of us squish close together while standing in front of the Quonset. The news reporter stood right in front of the big movie camera and held a microphone up to her mouth. She began speaking, but I was too nervous to hear any of the words. I was suddenly able to focus when she began talking directly to my brother, who was standing right beside me.

"Are you ready to get your wish?" She directed the microphone toward Clint.

Clint nodded. "Yeah!"

I could tell Clint was excited.

Just then, the man from the Make-A-Wish foundation rolled a shiny red three-wheeler out of the Quonset and presented it to Clint. The energy that radiated from all of us was enough to light up a whole house in the darkest of nights.

"Is this what you wanted?"

"It's just what I asked for." Clint quietly put his hands on the handles of the three-wheeler, seemingly in shock.

The reporter asked, "Why did you want this so bad?"

"Because I think it will be fun, and I can ride it down the field to help my dad and Grandpa when they need help with stuff. This way I can drive to the house quick and get them what they need and then take it back to them in a flash." Clint grinned.

"Are you ready to ride it?" The reporter still had the microphone in her hand.

"Yeah!" Clint shouted.

"Okay, climb on." The Make-A-Wish guy placed a white heavy plastic chest protector over Clint's head, followed by thick red gloves, and a shiny red helmet. He gave Clint a few instructions, then started the three-wheeler.

Within just a few minutes, Clint was driving away.

"And there he goes," someone said, and we all chuckled.

We watched him ride down the dirt road that led to the field. I started to wonder if he was ever going to come back.

"This is for you." The Make-A-Wish lady interrupted my thoughts as she handed me a pink teddy bear that had two hearts on its white belly.

"She's a Care Bear. Her name is Love-a-Lot."

I hugged it tight close to my chest.

"Your brother wanted you to have it."

I had only seen Care Bears advertised on TV and never dreamed of holding one of my own. My heart was so filled with gladness that words escaped me.

"And Cody, this one's for you."

Cody was still being held in Dad's arms. She handed him a Care Bear of his own. It was orange with two yellow flowers on its white belly.

"Your bear is named Friend Bear," she told him, and Cody started chewing on one of the bear's ears.

"Your bears have special powers," she explained to both of us. "Yours," she pointed to my bear, "spreads love and happiness wherever it goes. And yours," she pointed to Cody's bear, "spreads friendship wherever it goes."

The lady smiled a compassionate smile as she reminded us that they were a gift from Clint and how much he wanted us to have them. I squeezed my bear a little tighter, pouring my love into it on that cold November day.

We all stayed up late that night to watch ourselves on TV. Clint's Make-A-Wish story was aired on the ten o'clock news as a special report. In a time when TV shows and news stories weren't readily available on demand, we watched intently as the story unfolded before our eyes. The reporter, the Make-A-Wish Foundation people, and news anchors did such a good job explaining Clint's cancer battle in a short amount of time. They also helped to raise awareness of leukemia and testicular cancer, to generate support for the nonprofit organization, and to ignite hope. We all smiled, laughed, and reminisced about the day the story aired. Light had been emitted in the darkness, and the spark from the granted wish gave Clint the strength to continue fighting the battle.

The day Clint's wish came true. Fall 1984

29

LEARNING ABOUT MIRACLES

I WAS TOLD that faith wasn't something that our family always had. Instead, faith found us. Aside from battling leukemia, Clint had another life-altering incident take place. When he was seven years old, he hit his head on the monkey bars and wasn't expected to survive his brain injury. A miracle occurred, but nobody knew the extent of that miracle until several days after he had woke up from his coma.

Mom was sitting on a chair in the hospital with both Clint and three-year-old me on her lap. She had found a children's Bible in one of the hospital's waiting rooms and was reading a story from it, out loud to both of us, but more for herself. She seemed to be trying to come to grips with the miracle of Clint surviving his terrible fall.

After Mom had finished reading the story to us, she flipped through the pages of the book showing us the pictures when Clint suddenly called out, "Stop, that's the man!"

"What man?"

"The man who was in my room. The man who asked me if I wanted to live or die."

"Jesus?" Mom looked bewildered.

Clint was still pointing to the picture of the man. "I don't know his name; I just know that's the man who was in my room."

"When was he in your room?"

"When I was in that room that didn't have a TV in it. He was there with two other people."

Mom told us later that she was starting to make the connection. She realized he was referring to the ICU.

"What did he tell you?"

"He asked me if I wanted to live or die."

"Tell me more. What did he look like? Who were the two other people?" Mom had asked. She said she was trying to reason a logical explanation for Clint thinking he had seen Jesus.

"I was lying in that bed with my eyes closed, and my head hurt really bad. All of a sudden, I could see light everywhere. I opened my eyes, and there was a man—that man." He pointed to the picture of Jesus again. "He was at the end of my bed. He wasn't standing on the ground, though; he was kind of floating there, and he was wearing a white robe. There was white everywhere. There was a person on each side of him wearing white, too, but they didn't say anything. They were just with him, and their feet weren't touching the ground, either. It's like they had wings or something, but I didn't see any wings. The man had really bright blue eyes like I've never seen before. He floated there for a minute, then he talked to me."

"What did he say?"

"He asked me if I wanted to live or die. He said that I had two choices. One choice was that he'd make it so my head would stop hurting, and that I'd never be in pain again. The other choice was that I could stay and live with my family, but I'd still have to be in pain sometimes."

Mom asked quietly, "What did you tell him?"

"I told him that I wanted to stay with my family. I didn't care if I was hurting or not; I didn't want to leave my family."

"What did he say when you told him that?"

"He didn't say anything. He came over to me and put his hand on my head. Instantly, the pain was gone, and then he and the two other people disappeared. Maybe they were angels?"

Mom hadn't taken her eyes off Clint. "Then what happened?"

"I woke up and tried to talk. A nurse came into the room, and then the doctors. They took the tube out of my throat, and as soon as I was able to talk, I asked the nurse, 'Where's my TV?'"

Mom's eyes glistened. "Clint, you saw Jesus!"

"Who is Jesus?"

"This man!" Mom excitedly pointed to Jesus' picture.

"Oh," Clint kind of mumbled. "I didn't know his name."

We hadn't gone to church before this incident took place. There weren't any pictures of Jesus in our house. We didn't have any children's Bibles in our bedroom. My parents both believed in God, "A God," they would sometimes say, but they weren't sold on Jesus or even Christianity for that matter. They believed that there was some higher power in control of the universe, some explanation as to why bad things happened, and some justification as to why humans inhabited the Earth. They believed in a higher power because they just knew in their hearts that there had to be more to life than what they were able to see with their own eyes. They had to have something to hold onto on days when the world felt too heavy, but usually they just held onto each other.

It was in that moment in the hospital waiting room that Mom realized that Jesus was real and he had found us; we didn't go seeking him.

Jesus was alive!

"Let's go find your dad," Mom said calmly. I don't think she wanted to frighten us with how fast her heart was racing.

Once we found Dad, Mom had Clint tell him the story that he had just told us. Mom knew that kids could tell stories, so she wanted to know if Clint's story was real. Clint told the exact same story to our dad the same way that he had just told us.

Dad had been brought up in the Catholic religion and believed wholeheartedly in miracles, but the story that Clint had just told him almost brought him to his knees. The world started to make a little more sense to both my mom and dad. They now had something that they could both believe in. There was indeed a Jesus, and he had saved their son's life.

The questions still came, though. If Jesus could save his life and take his pain away, why didn't he take Clint's cancer away, too? Why did Clint still have to suffer so much throughout his life? Yes, a miracle took place, but why was Clint still sick?

When given a miracle, one can still have so many questions. Clint never had questions, though. His explanation was always the same.

"Jesus gave me the choice. He told me that I would still suffer if I chose to stay with my family."

Many times, I asked Clint to tell me more. To explain to me why Jesus didn't just make him all better. Why didn't he make everyone better? Clint felt in his heart that he had to suffer so that others could live. He felt that the trial drugs he was on would help doctors to find ways to cure other kids with cancer, and they did. The survival rate for childhood leukemia with children diagnosed with acute lymphoblastic leukemia (ALL) went from a five-year survival rate of ten percent in the 1970s to now, in 2026, a five-year survival rate of eighty-three percent. The survival rate for childhood testicular cancer has significantly increased as well.

Clint told the story of seeing Jesus to countless people. Most believed him, a few questioned him, and some didn't believe him at all. It used to upset me when people didn't believe my brother's story, and a few times it even led me to question his story. Faith is something that isn't always easy to hold onto. The older I grew, the more his story made sense to me, though. After all, at some point we all need something to believe in, something beyond seeing with our own eyes. Hope for tomorrow. Faith to carry us through. Belief that we are all on Earth together to serve a purpose higher than ourselves. Clint's story has not only taught me more about faith and Jesus, but it has taught me more about humanity itself.

EACH DAY IS A GIFT

~KIMBERLEY'S THOUGHT~

I WAS STANDING proudly next to my big brother in the light November rain, waiting for the bus to pick us up for school. The fall country air of damp grape leaves, wet almond tree bark, smoke lingering from close by fireplaces, and wet dirt surrounded just the two of us. We stood at the stop sign playing the Indian Bowl game with our feet. The dirt was a little more damp than normal. We both spun and spun around trying to make our bowl the deepest one of all. The bus arrived before we could measure them to see who the winner was, but I'm sure it was Clint.

My brother was still sick with cancer, but he was getting better. The treatments were working, and even his hair was starting to grow back again. It had been a rough year of treatments for him, missing school, and feeling awful. In a way, though, it made him stronger, enough to endure many more health trials throughout his entire life. I was just thankful that I didn't have to ride to school on the bus without him because standing at the stop sign by myself was no fun at all!

Clint and I rode to school on the big yellow bus with Mr. Beasley as our chauffeur. I was dropped off first, at Campus Park Elementary, but instead of running to the kindergarten playground, I ran off to where the bigger kids played. After all, I was now a big first grader. I had a new teacher that year, but I was still surrounded by the same friends, plus a few new ones, and the lunch card lady was still the same.

When I walked into the lunch room that day, I no longer felt the uneasy feeling while anticipating the lunch card lady's question of how my brother was doing. I smiled my friendliest smile with my eyes sparkling brightly as I approached her little wooden table and quietly handed her my lunch card. She took it from my hands and started to punch a hole in it as she asked me the usual question, "How is your brother doing?"

"Great!" I answered. "He rode the bus to school with me today."

"That's just wonderful, sweetheart, just wonderful." She smiled as she stood up from behind her little table and came close to me. She knelt beside me and pulled me into her arms, embracing me with the gentlest hug I'd ever felt, almost as if she was afraid to hug me, with fear that I might break. Tears were streaming down her face, but I didn't understand why. In a way, it felt as if she needed the hug from me more than I needed the hug from her. Adults were often hard to understand because they didn't always say what they were thinking.

"Have a good lunch!" she said as she stood up. She brushed the tears from her eyes and walked back to her seat behind the little wooden table.

"Thank you!" I replied, smiling a big toothless smile as I made my way through the little doorway to where the food was waiting for me.

I never did learn the name of the lunch card lady, but she, like so many others, played such an important role in helping to shape who I grew up to be, who I am. She showed me what compassion and understanding looked like without ever having to say much at all. She cared about my brother. She cared enough to ask me how he was every day that I saw her. I didn't know it then, but in a way, she must have cared about me, too. She touched my life, and I don't know for sure, but maybe I touched hers as well.

You see, to most people, Clint was a warrior, a fighter, a miracle. But to me, he was just my brother. The one who knew things that I would never fully understand. The one who'd been through things that I couldn't explain or even comprehend. The one who taught me to just live life! To take things as they were without questioning it all. The one who taught me how to embrace every moment of each day as if it were a special gift. A moment in time that will never come again.

People say that everything always works out like it's meant to, and the older I get, the more I believe that to be true. Often, it's not until after the moment has passed that we can look back and realize how everything fell into place as it should have. My childhood was exactly as it should have been.

The people that my family was surrounded by during those years of challenges and hardships are exactly the people who were supposed to be there, those who were meant to help us on the journey of life. Our family was also there for them. Touching countless lives that we will never know the impact of. After all, we are all just little fish in a big pond whose ripples of our lives splash into the lives of others and travel well beyond our ability to see. Each of us is one of God's angels, right here on Earth.

Doctors couldn't quite explain what happened over the months that followed Clint's wish being granted. They just knew that, once again, a miracle had occurred. Clint's cancer slowly disappeared, and he was put into remission. Knowing that his cancer could come back at any time was something that always lingered in our minds, but we never let it consume us. When worry hovered close, we held onto our faith. It wasn't something we could see, or even fully explain, but it was what we knew. Faith kept us strong and allowed us to see the joy in everything. For us, it wasn't always a feeling of happiness; instead, joy is what filled our hearts when we allowed ourselves to recognize all the good that surrounded us.

Clint is a warrior. An angel. *My* big brother. Someone who reminds me daily how amazing life is. Someone that I will always look up to. Clint continues to help countless people with his shining light; friends, family, and complete strangers. His strength and courage radiate into others like a beacon of hope in the night. My brother may have seen Jesus but me—I saw my brother and that's all the proof that I needed. You see, where I lived was a house filled with love and laughter. And even when I was far away, I always felt that I was near.

The End

EPILOGUE

WHEN I TURNED SEVEN, my dad, Gene, got a job teaching at juvenile hall in Merced and later quit his job working on the ranch. Though he still helped with harvest, irrigating, and other pressing ranch work whenever he could. Working at juvenile hall helped my dad to understand the lives and challenges that other families faced, and that those were much different than our own. He later went on to get his teaching credential and taught hundreds of students many life lessons throughout his teaching career of twenty plus years. Throughout his life, he was a baseball coach, teacher, mentor, bus driver, devoted husband, compassionate father, and many other things.

My mom, Betty, took on the job as a truant officer for the middle school in Livingston when Cody started kindergarten. In that line of work, she learned the challenges of many other families in our small community. She embraced them and grew close to the students that she worked with. She later went on to graduate from college with her teaching credential at the age of forty, inspiring many that it's never too late to give up on your dreams. My mom spent several years teaching junior high math and science, touching the lives of many. Though she officially retired from teaching in her sixties, she continues to work. She spreads love and joy to others through the dreamcatchers, blankets, and other works of art that she creates with her own two hands.

My little brother, Cody, continues to keep everyone laughing with his quick wit and fun-loving personality. After high school, he went on to college at the University of Nevada Reno, where he became the first Wolfie in UNR history to be the mascot all four years of his college experience. He graduated from UNR with his teaching credential, wearing his Wolfie shoes to accept his diploma. He then went on to become a volunteer firefighter in a small town in Nevada while also balancing being a full-time junior high English teacher. Cody later moved to the state of Louisiana, where he continues to touch the lives of many.

The circle of people that I was surrounded by in my younger years influenced me to carry on the desire to help others. From the moment, with the help of my dear friend Donna Grunloh, that I learned how to draw a star on a child's paper, I knew that I was meant to be a teacher. I had others later in life, as well as my parents, who continued to remind me of that dream. I graduated with honors from California State University Stanislaus the same year that I was married to my supportive husband. I finally reached my dream of becoming a full-time teacher when I was in my early twenties. I taught first and second grade at a public school in Nevada for seventeen years before becoming an independently contracted tutor and teacher. I continue to follow my passion for teaching by encouraging children all over the world to find their strengths.

Clint's story is not over. He continues to fight daily health battles. He relapsed again when he was twelve years old, but with advances in medicine and the help of experimental drugs, he was in remission again within a year. He was finally considered completely cancer-free at the age of seventeen. For the first time since he was four years old, his monthly check-ups turned into yearly ones. After five years of having a clean bill of health, he no longer had to go back for leukemia or testicular cancer screenings.

When Clint was eighteen years old, doctors determined that because of his head injury, the prolonged use of chemotherapy, radiation, steroids, and other cancer drugs, he would have permanent brain damage. He was also diagnosed with short-term memory loss. A disability that he continues to struggle with.

A side-effect from the prolonged radiation led Clint to deal with another bout of cancer in 2003. It was then that he was diagnosed with sarcoma cancer in his face. He again was given a very grim diagnosis, but he fought with every fiber of his being and defied all the odds. He has been officially cancer-free since 2005 and continues the daily struggle of being mentally disabled, with short-term memory loss, and the physical scars that have left weakness in parts of his body and deformities on his face.

The life lessons that Clint's childhood cancer battle taught us helped our family deal with many more battles that we would later face. Papa gathered strength from our family during his fight with liver cancer. My Grandma Ghiggia leaned on all of us for support during her bought with breast cancer. My mom kept up her courage and hope during her struggle with stage four ovarian cancer, another miracle I'll write about one day. My cousin Marina was diligent with her follow-up visits after her diagnosis with breast cancer. My Aunt Londa relied on faith during both her struggle with surviving open-heart surgery and her experience with colon cancer. All our family got answers together when my Grandma Pierce was diagnosed with Alzheimer's. My Aunt Linda had questions answered by my parents while dealing with breast cancer and later passed from ovarian cancer.

Lastly, our family gathered strength and faith from each other after my dad's diagnosis with Glioblastoma brain cancer; a hard-fought battle that he lost.

Cancer is an awful thing to bear, to witness, to be a part of. But in some ways, cancer is also a blessing; it's what brought our family close to each other. It's what taught us how to cherish each day as if it were our last. It brought people into our lives that we may have never otherwise met. It's what showed us what true friendship looks like. It's what taught us that in all things, good can be found. It's what taught us to never stop living!

ABOUT THE AUTHOR

KIMBERLEY GHIGGIA THORN was raised in small country communities in the Central Valley of California. After marrying and moving to Nevada, she taught elementary grades in the public-school classroom for seventeen years. Later, working from home, she became a private teacher for children, with students all over the world. She now spends much of her teaching time focusing on helping young learners find joy in writing.

When Kimberley is not teaching, she enjoys reading, writing, playing guitar, taking long walks with her dogs, and helping her husband with chores on their small farm. She loves to travel and explore nature, spending as much time as she can doing both.

Kimberley is thankful for each day and finds joy in living life to its fullest.

www.ingramcontent.com/pod-product-compliance
Lightning Source LLC
Chambersburg PA
CBHW060523160726
47991CB00001B/155